Documents and Debates
British Social and Economic History 1800–1900

Documents and Debates
General Editor: John Wroughton M.A., F.R.Hist.S.

British Social and Economic History 1800 — 1900

Neil Tonge and Michael Quincey

Published by
PALGRAVE MACMILLAN
Houndmills, Basingstoke, Hampshire RG21 6XS and
175 Fifth Avenue, New York, N.Y. 10010
Companies and representatives throughout the world

PALGRAVE MACMILLAN is the global academic imprint of the Palgrave
Macmillan division of St. Martin's Press, LLC and of Palgrave Macmillan Ltd.
Macmillan® is a registered trademark in the United States, United Kingdom
and other countries. Palgrave is a registered trademark in the European
Union and other countries.

ISBN 0–333–27452–0

This book is printed on paper suitable for recycling and
made from fully managed and sustained forest sources.

A catalogue record for this book is available from the British Library.

Printed and bound in Great Britain by
Antony Rowe Ltd, Chippenham and Eastbourne

Contents

Acknowledgements

The authors and publishers wish to thank the following who have kindly given permission for the use of copyright material:

George Allen & Unwin (Publishers) Ltd for an extract from *The Development of British Industry and Foreign Competition 1875 – 1914* by D. Aldcroft; Associated British Publishers Ltd for extracts from *English Historical Documents*, Vol. XI, 1783 – 1832, by Aspinall and Smith, published by Eyre and Spottiswoode (Publishers) Ltd and *Money – Riches and Poverty* by L. G. Chiozza published by Methuen and Co. Ltd; B. T. Batsford Ltd for an extract from *The Agricultural Revolution 1750 – 1880* by J. D. Chambers and G. E. Mingay; Professor Mark Blaug and the Economic History Association for an extract from 'The Myth of the Old Poor Law and the Making of the New' published in *Journal of Economic History*, Vol. 23, 1963; BBC Publications for an extract from *Milestones in Working Class History* by N. Longmate; Frank Cass & Co. Ltd for extracts from *The Philosophy of Manufactures* . . . . (1835) by Andrew Ure, *History of the Chartist Movement* (1854) by R. G. Gamage, *High Farming under Liberal Covenants the Best Substitute for Protection* (1848) by James Caird and *English Agriculture in 1850 – 1851* (1852) by James Caird; The Economic History Society for extracts from '*The Standard of Living during the Industrial Revolution: A Discussion*' by E. J. Hobsbawm and R. M. Hartwell in *The Economic History Review*, 2nd Series, Vol XVI (1963); 'The Making of the English Working Class?' by R. M. Hartwell and R. Currie in *The Economic History* Review, 2nd Series, XVIII (1965); 'Did Victorian Britain Fail?' by D. M. Closkey, in *The Economic History Review*, 2nd Series, XXIII (1970); 'British Industrial Growth, 1873 – 96: A Balanced View' by A. E. Musson in *The Economic History Review*, 2nd Series, XVIII (1964); Victor Gollancz Ltd for extracts from *The Making of the English Working Class* by E. P. Thompson; The Hamlyn Publishing Group Ltd for an extract from *Victorian Cities* by Asa Briggs; D. C. Heath & Company for an extract from *The Industrial Revolution in Britain: Triumph or Disaster* by P. A. M. Taylor; Croom Helm Ltd for extracts from *The New Economic History of the Railways* by Patrick O'Brien, and *Essays in Labour History* edited by Briggs and MacMillan; David Higham Associates Ltd on behalf of E. J. Hobsbawm for an extract from *Industry and Empire* published by Penguin Books Ltd; Leicester University Press for an extract from *The Railway Interest* by G. Alderman; Longman Group Ltd for an extract from *The Bleak Age* by Hammond and Hammond; Oxford University Press for extracts from *Victorian England, Portrait of an Age* by G. M. Young (2nd edition 1953) and *British Economy of the Nineteenth Century* by W. W. Rostow (1948); Penguin Books Ltd for extracts from *A History of the Cost of Living* by J. Burnett and *Chartism and the Chartists* by David Jones; A. D. Peters & Co. on behalf of Peter Mathias for an extract from *The First Industrial Nation* published by Methuen and Co. Ltd; Routledge & Kegan Paul Ltd for an extract from *English Landed Society in the Nineteenth Century* by F. N. J. Thompson; Routledge & Kegan Paul Ltd and University of Toronto Press for an extract from *Principles of Political Economy* by J. S. Mill (editor J. M. Robson) in the series *Collected Works of John Stuart Mill* (general editor, F. E. L. Priestley); Weidenfeld (Publishers) Ltd for extracts from *Early Victorian Government* by Oliver MacDonagh and *Industrial Retardation in Britain* by A. L. Levine; Edith Whetham for an extract from *History of British Agriculture 1846 – 1914* (1971).

Every effort has been made to trace all the copyright holders but if any have been inadvertently overlooked the publishers will be pleased to make the necessary arrangement at the first opportunity.

Cover illustration reproduced by kind permission of the *Illustrated London News*.

The authors wish to extend special thanks to the following: for practical help and encouragement, Mr C. Winlow, Newcastle upon Tyne LEA Adviser in Geography and History; the clerical staff at Pendower Teachers' Centre, Newcastle upon Tyne; for helpful comment, Mr T. Gwynne, History tutor, Newcastle upon Tyne Polytechnic; and Mr J. Gulson, senior teacher, Durham.

General Editor's Preface

This book forms part of a series entitled *Documents and Debates*, which is aimed primarily at the sixth form. Each volume covers approximately one century of either British or European history and consists of up to ten sections, each dealing with a major theme. In most cases a varied selection of documents will bring evidence to bear on the chosen theme, supplemented by a stimulating extract from a modern historian. A few 'Debate' sections, however, will centre on the most important controversies of each century. Here extracts from the changing opinions of modern research, normally found only in learned journals and expensive monographs, will be made available in manageable form. The series intends partly to provide experience for those pupils who are required to answer questions on documentary extracts at 'A' Level, and partly to provide pupils of all abilities with a digestible and interesting collection of source material, which will extend the normal textbook approach.

This book is designed essentially for the pupil's own personal use. The authors' introduction will put the century as a whole into perspective, highlighting the central issues, main controversies, available source material and recent developments. Although it is clearly not our intention to replace the traditional textbook, each section will carry its own brief introduction, which will set the documents into context. The short, select bibliography is intended to encourage the pupil to follow up issues raised in the section by further reading – without being subjected to the off-putting experience of an exhaustive list. A wide variety of source material has been used in order to give the pupils the maximum amount of experience – letters, speeches, newspapers, memoirs, diaries, official papers, Acts of Parliament, Minute Books, accounts, local documents, family papers etc. The questions vary in difficulty, but aim throughout to compel the pupil to think in depth by the use of unfamiliar material. Historical knowledge and understanding will be tested, as well as basic comprehension. Pupils will also be encouraged by the questions to assess the reliability of evidence, to recognise bias and emotional prejudice, to reconcile conflicting accounts and to extract the essential from the irrelevant. Some questions, marked with an asterisk, require knowledge outside the immediate extract and are intended for further research or discussion, based on the pupil's general knowledge of the period. Finally, we hope the students using this material will learn something of the nature of historical inquiry and the role of the historian.

John Wroughton

Introduction

Administration of the unforeseen

Between 1750 and 1850 Britain went through a series of changes in
industrial technology, organisation of labour, finance of business operations and methods of goods distribution which is commonly called the
'Industrial Revolution'. The population of England and Wales doubled
between 1800 and 1850 and almost doubled again between 1850 and
1900. Large sections of the population were grouped together in
conurbations, so that periods of prosperity, such as 1850–70, and slump,
like the 'Hungry Forties', were experienced with a new immediacy. The
problems thrown up and highlighted by the fluctuations of the
industrialised economy demanded action in response. This volume is
concerned with the response to the effects of the Industrial Revolution:
the response of government, of society in general, of particular groups
within society and of individuals. Sometimes their reactions coincided, at
others they varied and conflicted. The results of their interaction, for
good or ill, determined the new socio-political shape of Britain in 1900.

The reader is not dealing, therefore, with a primer covering every
aspect of social and economic history of the nineteenth century. In fact,
such coverage would be impossible in such a short space, except in a
cursory fashion which in itself would be meaningless. We intend this
book to be used against the background of the standard secondary sources
on the period and have deliberately chosen response to the Industrial
Revolution as a basis for the selection of contemporary sources to
illustrate the main difficulties in dealing with primary evidence. As far as
possible, the section introductions attempt to give context and perspective, where contemporary developments, controversies, or issues are
covered, while the main areas and strands of debate are outlined in those
sections where current academic debates are analysed. The documents
following each introduction are arranged in an order which fits the
outlined context or analysis. The sections run in chronological order,
beginning with the standard of living and potential for revolution at the
start of the century, concluding with the 'Great Depression' and overall
assessment at the end of the century. The intervening sections, three to
eight, deal with topics that span the period.

The nineteenth century saw the social and economic transformation of

Britain, the fundamental change begun by the Industrial Revolution worked out in both direct and indirect response to the commercial and manufacturing miracle. Despite the assimilation of 'Industrial Revolution' into the language of the historian, its interpretation has been the subject of intense debate. No longer is it accepted as a simplified episode as described in 1901 by Beard, 'Suddenly almost like a thunderbolt from a clear sky were ushered in the storm and stress of Industrial Revolution.'[1] Economists have provided theories of growth which point to an evolutionary process at work. W. W. Rostow wrote of a 'take-off into self sustained growth' in order to illustrate the preconditions necessary for the economy of a country to be described as industrialised. Productive investment and leading sectors within the economy had to be identified and methods of quantitative analysis brought to bear in historical research. This still poses difficulties, for the collection of statistics is a recent development. The census was only begun in 1801 and was barely reliable until 1841. Modern government finds unemployment an albatross about its neck yet such figures were not available until 1921. Thus, earlier than the nineteenth century the picture darkens and images remain incomplete. To complicate the issue further, historians argue about the validity of qualitative judgements and quantitative evidence and whether quantitative judgement can be soundly based on qualitative evidence. Causation is a debate in itself and raises the related issue of dating the Revolution. Was it 1780–1830 or 1800–50? The debate continues and will do so as new evidence emerges, fresh research is published and old evidence re-evaluated. Such is the essence of history.

The response of contemporaries, in whatever capacity, is central to the understanding of nineteenth-century social and economic history. Often, the response is the main indicator that otherwise imperceptible change was taking place. Equally, the response can reveal attitudes and motivation which enable the historian to provide explanation. Modern students are sometimes surprised by the length of time it took nineteenth-century government to act, or by the limited nature of the action itself. We automatically look to government to legislate, the nineteenth century expected government to rule. Thus, the role of government reluctant to embark on state intervention is underlined throughout the book. This helps to explain why the century is well endowed with crusading individuals and pinpoints alternative action to legislation by other groups outside parliament. Gradually, the enormity of the problems raised by Britain's rapid industrialisation were recognised and state intervention increased to meet these needs. It is important to remember that contemporaries were acutely conscious of the issue of state intervention and that the debate of collectivism versus individualism was hotly contested, both philosophically and practically, throughout the period.

Economic trends are frightening, impersonal forces to those who find themselves on the negative receiving end. Not surprisingly, the reactions in such circumstances are bewilderment and bitterness. The indication that the Industrial Revolution was well under way by the end of the Napoleonic Wars is the plight of certain handicraft workers. This is manifest in the frustrated machine breaking of Big Enoch, widespread formation of secret combinations and the marches of the Blanketeers. Such phenomena have provoked the debate on the standard of living of the working classes and the emergence of two historical schools of thought on the subject, illustrating again the difficulty of achieving concrete conclusions from inadequate evidence.

What is clear, however, is that society was responding to the change occasioned by technological advance. The frustration felt by workers was expressed violently in certain districts. Government was alarmed by the form of expression in the political context of the time, fearing political revolution and employing credulous agents to report to a secret parliamentary committee. Radicals like Hunt were quick to exploit the situation. Others like Place were content to proceed by polite lobbying. through normal channels. As always, there were victims, as at St. Peter's Fields in Manchester, where cavalry rode down peaceful civilians because a local magistrate was convinced that he had a riot on his hands. Such were the first, blind responses to change which was being experienced yet not understood. How far political revolution was a figment of the imagination of the rulers and how far it was a definite goal of combinations, demonstrators or agitators is another area of debate.

Combinations, unions of skilled workmen formed to protect their own interests, were the direct result of Industrial Revolution. Skilled craftsmen could no longer look forward to becoming masters or senior journeymen in time and could only foresee employment as a skilled hand for their working life. In order to protect their interests many 'combined' within their workshops to safeguard their standing within the trade, if necessary against their employer. Their motives appear innocent enough today. Their emergence coincided with a period of political instability and they were outlawed. By the end of the Napoleonic Wars many combinations existed in spite of proscription and they appeared the more sinister because of their secrecy. It says much for the healthy Radical tradition inherent in British politics by this time that their legality could be achieved by Francis Place and Joseph Hume through parliament.

By 1830 symptoms of industrialisation were too pressing to be ignored. Government was to produce the Great Reform Act of 1832, implement the Poor Law Commission, take the first tentative step towards involvement in Education and expand factory legislation. It is no coincidence that the same period saw the emergence of recognisable Trade Unions, the product of intelligent working men in the urban context seeking to protect their skills and value of labour. The Utopianism of Owen's Grand National Consolidated Trades Union was a failure and guaranteed that the future organisation of labour would proceed along particular trade lines and by local co-operative organisation. The G.N.C.T.U. appeared at a time of conservative reaction to unionism and was defenceless as economic recession set in. Those who ruled identified unionism in the same category as the ill-fated Chartist movement, mistakenly certainly, but it resulted in the carefully moderate progress of Trade Unions until the Royal Commission of 1867. Unionists were at pains to point out by then, as the London Trades Council made clear, 'We have no desire to make our societies channels for political agitation.' Trade Unionism had been sired by the Industrial Revolution and was the response of skilled craftsmen to hitherto unforeseen industrial relations. However, it never quite lost the taint of having its origin in a period of political (albeit foreign) upheaval. Just as labour responded, so did masters and government. To many, organised labour was as big a threat to individual liberty as was state intervention in society.

The role of the state was a question which occupied contemporaries of the nineteenth century and which has produced among historians the debate over 'laissez-faire': the idea that it was not the job of government to interfere in social and economic relationships between groups and/or individuals; that, if left alone, society and the economy would adjust themselves satisfactorily. It is a wide-ranging argument covering the whole century. It was a stated philosophical principle: J. S. Mill wrote that it ought to be 'the general practice'. Support for it spread across the political spectrum. There is a danger of interpreting the term too narrowly, tying it to economic policy only. It can also be used as a generalisation of little meaning to cover complexity. What the student must gauge and decide is its real influence on the attitudes of contemporaries. Other philosophies and influences were at work on society and among politicians. Novel problems demanded novel solutions and forced state intervention: the poor, factories, public health, education, electoral reform, agriculture and railways. Industrialisation had borne urbanisation, out of which was turned a social fabric of a weave and texture not seen before. The anguish caused to conservatives by the repeal of the Corn Laws, the vehement argument against factory and health legislation, the heart searching of government involving itself increasingly in education are all testimony to the fact that government was painfully aware of setting possibly dangerous precedents. When the State did intervene, therefore, it did so only to provide the necessary stability for society to function in the accepted manner, in order to allow the optimum interplay of individual enterprise consistent with personal liberty. Such concentrated effort to avoid collectivism demands that 'laissez-faire' be considered and interpreted meaningfully and not be dismissed as too broad a concept or as an encouragement to error in historical research.

The forces unleashed on British society by the Industrial Revolution were vast and inexorable. Their effects are the subject of disputation. What did the shift from agrarian to urban industrial society mean for agriculture? During the initial stages of the Industrial Revolution methods of farming remained ostensibly unchanged, but land usage did not. A new era of enclosures began which added to the dislocation of rural society, if only in certain areas. To be a farmer at the beginning of the nineteenth century meant prosperity as England fed itself and financed war against the French. The bubble burst after the Congress of Vienna in 1815, yet production of wheat rose steadily up to 1835. Why, then, did some contemporaries talk in terms of economic disaster after 1815? The repeal of the Corn Laws did not produce the débâcle expected by many a wealthy landowner. Instead, agriculture continued into a period of prosperity, successfully feeding industrial society. By the turn of the century, however, changes in the shape and character of agriculture in England were evident: fewer worked on the land and the golden age of profits had vanished in the face of imported meat and wheat.

Just what difference did the railways make to the quality of everyday life? Between 1825 and 1848 approximately 4500 miles of railway track were laid in England and Wales. By 1870 there were over 13 000 miles. It is surely no accident that the rapid growth of railways coincided with massively increased output of coal, iron and steel. Yet the accurate assessment of the difference made by the railways to society in terms of facilitating provision of goods, means of personal travel and such things as holidays is difficult and necessitates detailed and specific study.

How often did contemporaries really understand the stimuli to which they responded? It has been argued that the Great Depression at the end of the century was a myth. The investment levels in industry were maintained, while the volume of British trade and output rose, as did the tonnage of British shipping, right up to 1914. Yet by the end of the century a Royal Commission had been convened to investigate 'The Depression in Trade and Industry'. In fact, the profits being made were not consistent with the levels to which investors had been accustomed from the period when Britain was the workshop of the world. Foreign competition was catching up and proving more adaptable to new techniques while Britain still relied on its staple industries and tried technology. In retrospect, the historian finds it relatively easy to explain the paradox of depression amidst ostensible prosperity. Is it more important to recognise, however, that some contemporaries were convinced that they were caught in a massive depression and that this revived the protectionist lobby and had ramifications for twentieth-century economic and social policy?

By the turn of the century the butterfly of industrial society had struggled from its chrysalis. What kind of creature was it? The views of contemporaries vary: some saw a beautiful, efficient being, well proportioned and sure of its environment. Others saw a pallid travesty of beauty, spotted with soot and grime, wings tattered by hard brick and unyielding iron, unable to feed adequately in its harsh environment and so unable to fulfil its true potential. Which picture was more accurate? Was Britain in the process of building a new Jerusalem or busily creating a new Gehenna? More importantly for the historian, what did the people of the time think they were doing?

More and more the student must learn to seek the primary source, to establish what contemporaries felt to be certainties, to acknowledge bias but to realise that, like all men, they acted on their convictions, prejudices, false assumptions, assessments and all. By so doing, the historian can begin to enter the minds of his subjects. Social and economic history is concerned with people and their behaviour. The documents contained in this book offer a taste of people wrestling with forces and problems and shaping the world in which they lived. The Victorian opponents of radical constitutional reform who felt that, 'Our stability is but balance, and wisdom lies in masterful administration of the unforeseen', intuitively sensed the metamorphosis experienced by Britain in the nineteenth century. The metamorphosis happened without violent revolution but not without pain. The documents and extracts which follow ought to lead to possible answers to the essential questions of 'How' and 'Why'.

1   C. Beard, *The Industrial Revolution* (London, Allen & Unwin, 1901)

I The Standard of Living Debate

Introduction

Whether the standard of living of the labouring classes rose or fell during the initial stages of the Industrial Revolution is, of all the controversies of this period, the hardest fought. Yet, on the surface, there seems to be no argument against the fact that the national income per capita doubled between 1791 – 1851. This would naturally lead us to assume that the standard of living of the mass of the people improved. However, one needs to know:

1 the proportion of national income diverted from consumption to investment, which, in turn, depends on:
2 what proportion of consumption was going to property owners (rents and profits) and how much to workers (wages and salaries).

The debate dates from contemporaries of the early Industrial Revolution. Opinions even appear in nineteenth-century literature and the question is bedevilled by the tracts of the defenders and opponents of capitalism.

It is now possible, however, to identify two conflicting schools of thought on the subject, categorised as 'pessimists' and 'optimists'. The pessimists have a long pedigree opposed to the harsh and dehumanising aspects of industrialisation. E. P. Thompson and E. J. Hobsbawm are modern representatives of the pessimistic view. For the optimists, Sir John Clapham and T. S. Ashton, and more recently R. M. Hartwell, claim that the vast majority benefited in terms of falling prices, regular employment, and a wider range of employment opportunities.

The following points should always be borne in mind:

1 The major problem is in defining the period concerned. Some historians refer to 1780 – 1830, others to 1800 – 1850. The general conclusions drawn from the first period could be substantially different from the latter.
2 How does the historian define the 'average worker' for the period? In the 1841 census, for example, 1222 subdivisions are enumerated for cotton manufacture alone.
3 Increased material living standard can entail loss of security or status.
4 There are difficulties in compiling wages and prices indices to determine real wages.
5 A change in money wages may affect only a section of the working

classes. Furthermore, wages do not take into account periods of unemployment or short-time working.

It is thus easy to see how definite conclusions are so elusive.

1 The Components of the Debate

Controversy about working-class living standards in the Industrial Revolution reflects in part uncertainties in the evidence. In part it reflects ideological presuppositions among modern writers . . . .

5   It is a pronounced modern tendency to emphasise the business system, to analyse factors of growth, and to assume that, since in the long run all was justified by results, it is a calm understanding of technical development that is required. Such historians, in a sense, are studying a closed economic order: Ashton, for example, is prone to argue that it was politicians, with their erroneous laws and disturbing wars, who pre-
10   vented the entrepreneurs from demonstrating more quickly the benefits of the new industrial system. Within the limits of imperfect data, such an approach answers some questions very well. Yet the limits must be emphasised. We know little of unemployment or underemployment. We know too little about working class consumption: did most workers
15   really use the manufactured goods whose prices demonstrably fell, or even consume the meat and other foodstuffs about which historians argue? We know remarkably little about the distribution of national income; and some modern conclusions are of the order of 'it must have been', 'can we doubt that', or 'it is my guess'.

P. A. M. Taylor, *The Industrial Revolution in Britain. Triumph or Disaster*, Introduction p x

Questions

a   According to the author, what two major complications does the standard of living controversy contain (lines 1 – 3)?

b   Why does he think that a purely quantitative approach is limited (lines 7 – 8)?

c   From what the writer says about Ashton's theory, how can you tell that Ashton was an optimist (lines 8 – 11)?

d   What three major areas does the writer identify as being in need of greater clarification (lines 12 – 18)?

*   e   Analyse the factors which would support the view that the standard of living in Britain rose/declined between 1800 – 50.

2 Danger of Confusing the Evidence: Quality or Quantity?

From food we are led to homes, from homes to health, from health to family life, and thence to leisure, work discipline, education and play, intensity of labour, and so on. From standard-of-life we pass to way-of-life. But the two are not the same. The first is a measurement of quantities; the second a description (and sometimes an evaluation) of qualities. Where statistical evidence is appropriate to the first, we must rely largely upon 'literary evidence' as to the second. A major source of confusion arises from the drawing of conclusions to one from evidence appropriate only to the other. It is at times as if statisticians have been arguing: 'the indices reveal an increased per capita consumption of tea, sugar, meat and soap, therefore the working class was happier', while social historians have replied: 'the literary sources show that people were unhappy, therefore their standard of living must have deteriorated'.

E. P. Thompson, *The Making of the English Working Class*, 1966, p 230

Questions

a What factors does Thompson identify as being necessary areas of investigation in the working man's life (lines 1–4)?

b What important differentiation of category of factors does he underline (lines 4–5)?

c Explain what you think he means by 'statistical evidence' and 'literary evidence' (lines 6–7).

d For what common reason does he condemn many statisticians and social historians (lines 7–9)?

* *e* What picture of the condition of the working man is revealed by the literary evidence?

3 A Contemporary Account: the Pessimist

Debased alike by ignorance and pauperism, they have discovered, with the savage, what is the minimum of the means of life, upon which existence may be prolonged . . . . Prolonged and exhausting labour, continued from day to day, and from year to year, is not calculated to develop the intellectual or moral faculties of man . . . . To condemn man to such severity of toil is, in some measure, to cultivate in him the habits of an animal . . . . He neglects the comforts and delicacies of life. He lives in squalid wretchedness, on meagre food, and expends his superfluous gains on debauchery . . . .

The comparatively innutritious qualities of these articles of diet* are most evident. We are, however, by no means prepared to say that an individual living in a healthy atmosphere, and engaged in active employment in the open air, would not be able to continue protracted and severe labour, without any suffering, whilst nourished by this food . . . . But the population nourished on this aliment is crowded into one dense mass, in cottages separated by narrow, unpaved, and almost

* oatmeal and potatoes

pestilential streets; in an atmosphere loaded with the smoke and exhalations of a large manufacturing city. The operatives are congregated in rooms and workshops during twelve hours of the day, in an enervating
20 heated atmosphere, which is frequently loaded with dust or filaments of cotton, and impure from constant respiration, or from other causes . . . .

But the wages of certain classes are exceedingly meagre. The introduction of the power loom, though ultimately destined to be productive of the greatest general benefits, has, in the present restricted
25 state of commerce, occasioned some temporary embarrassment, by diminishing the demand for certain kinds of labour, and, consequently, their price. The hand-loom weavers, existing in the state of transition, still continue a very extensive class, and though they labour fourteen hours and upwards daily, earn only from five to seven shillings per week.

J. P. Kay-Shuttleworth, *The Moral and Physical Condition of the Working Classes employed in the Cotton Manufacture in Manchester*, 1832, pp 6—72

Questions

a According to Kay-Shuttleworth what is the basic result of ignorance and poverty (lines 7—8)?

b What effect has he observed as a result of (a) when extra money is earned (lines 8—9)?

c What effect do you think the working and living conditions described would have on the health of the people?

d How did industrialisation affect wages (lines 22—9)?

* e What important factor has Kay-Shuttleworth identified which influences the effects of the new technology (lines 24—5)? Investigate the importance of this factor in the English economy 1800—50.

* f Do you think this description is typical of early nineteenth-century industrialisation?

4   A Contemporary Account: the Optimist

Good workmen would have advanced their condition to that of overlookers, managers, and partners in new mills, and have increased at the same time the demand for their companions' labour in the market. It is only by an undisturbed progression of this kind that the rate of wages
5 can be permanently raised or upheld . . . .

Ill-usage of any kind is a very rare occurrence . . . .

In an establishment for spinning or weaving cotton, all the hard work is performed by the steam engine, which leaves for the attendant no hard labour at all . . . .

10 Occupations which are assisted by steam-engines require for the most part a higher . . . species of labour than those which are not; the exercise of the mind being then partially substituted for that of the muscles, constituting skilled labour, which is always paid more highly than

unskilled. On this principle we can readily account for the comparatively
high wages which the inmates of a cotton factory, whether children or
adults, obtain . . . .

By reducing the hours of labour, and thereby the amount of
subsistence derivable from the less objectionable occupations, they would
cause a corresponding increase in the competition for employment in the
more objectionable ones, and thus inflict an injury on the whole
labouring community, by wantonly renouncing the fair advantages of
their own . . . .

The factory system then, instead of being detrimental to the comfort of
the labouring population, is its grand Palladium . . . .

> Andrew Ure, *The Philosophy of Manufactures, or, an Exposition of
> the Scientific, Moral, and Commercial Economy of the Factory System
> of Great Britain*, 1835, pp 278–388

Questions

a   How does Ure maintain that the factory system ought to benefit the
conscientious worker and labour in general (lines 1 – 5)?

b   According to Ure, how has the factory improved the lot of the
workman (lines 7 – 9)?

c   Why is Ure not in favour of reduced working hours (lines 17 – 22)?

*   d   Write a critical response to Ure's arguments.

5 An Assessment of Quality: the Industrial Slum

But all the while Industrialism had been coming over England like a
climatic change; the French wars masked the consequences till they
became almost unmanageable. It is possible to imagine, with Robert
Owen, an orderly evolution of the rural village into the industrial
township, given the conditions which he enjoyed at New Lanark, a
limited size and a resident, paternal employer . . . . But any possibility of
a general development along these lines had already been lost in the
change-over from water to steam power, in the consequent growth of the
great urban aggregates, and the visible splitting of society, for which the
enclosures had created a rural precedent, into possessors and proletariat.
The employers were moving into the country; their officials followed
them into the suburbs; the better workmen lived in the better streets; the
mixed multitude of labour, native or Irish, was huddled in slums and
cellars, sometimes newly run up by speculative builders, sometimes, like
the labyrinth round Soho and Seven Dials, deserted tenements of the
upper classes . . . .

But the imagination can hardly apprehend the horror in which
thousands of families a hundred years ago were born, dragged out their
ghastly lives, and died: the drinking water brown with faecal particles,
the corpses kept unburied for a fortnight in a festering London August;

mortified limbs quivering with maggots; courts where not a weed would grow, and sleeping dens afloat with sewage.

G. M. Young, *Victorian England, Portrait of an Age*, 1936, pp 22—3

Questions

a What does Young think was the major effect of the Napoleonic Wars (lines 1—3)?

b What did industrialism do to English society (lines 8—10)?

c What important observation has Young made to which modern historians involved in the standard of living debate ought to pay attention (lines 11—16)?

d What did Young feel about the standard of living of the unskilled town worker (lines 17—22)?

* e Upon what type of evidence do you think Young has based his picture?

6   The Pessimist's Account – Hobsbawm

The Industrial Revolution did not merely replace cottage or slum workshop by factory, but multiplied *both* domestic industry and factories; the former either in direct dependence on the latter (as in cotton weaving), or in the rapidly expanding branches of production as yet quite untouched
5   by the factory (as in the garment industry), or in industries whose scale remained small even when they adopted new power. It also eventually killed off many of the expanded domestic industries it had created. The fate of these vastly expanded and then sacrificed domestic branches is therefore just as much a part of the social impact of the industrial
10 revolution as the fate of the factory population. It is entirely illegitimate to reject the half-million or more handloom weavers of 1830 or the army of seamstresses as survivals from pre-industrialism. But for the Industrial Revolution most of them would not have been there, or at any rate their life would have been very different.
15 Moreover, domestic industry in this new phase was – at least after its early boom – probably much less attractive than before the revolution, even setting aside extreme cases such as the slow strangulation of the handloom weavers . . . .

However, to compare the pre-industrial with the industrial age in
20 purely quantitative terms is to play Lear without the King . . . . In other words, poverty and dirt *alone* are not the issue. The change from one way of life to another is equally at stake. But while the careful student of poverty can only say that the case for deterioration, while not implausible, cannot be proved, though that against a marked improve-
25 ment is extremely strong, the sociological argument for deterioration is far more powerful . . . .

As is often the case, the poets saw things which the vulgar economists did not, and those who stammered their sense that the world was upside down were sometimes more correct than those who formulated their ideas lucidly. Charles Dickens, whose criticism of Coketown . . . was not merely that its inhabitants were poor and economically insecure, but that it was *inhuman*, expressed the anguish of a generation more profoundly than those who might merely have observed, with justice, that its drains were defective and something ought to be done about it. The historian forgets at his peril that the problem of the social impact of the industrial revolution is not whether men live by white or brown bread, no meat or roast beef; even though it can be shown that in our period it did not actually give them any extra roast beef. It is also, that men do not live by bread alone.

> E. J. Hobsbawm, 'The Standard of Living during the Industrial Revolution: A Discussion', *Economic History Review*, Vol 16, August 1963, pp 119–34

Questions

a   Explain in your own words the substance of Hobsbawm's first paragraph.

b   What important effect did the Revolution have on domestic industry (lines 2–6)?

c   On what basis does Hobsbawm think a comparison of pre-industrial with industrial society should be made (lines 19–21)?

d   In what respect does Hobsbawm feel that literary evidence is particularly valuable (lines 27–39)?

* e   Upon which handicraft trades did the Industrial Revolution have a disastrous effect?

7   The Pessimist's Case Criticised – Hartwell

Dr Hobsbawm twice claims that the eighteenth century is 'unknown' and that 'in the present state of our knowledge', comparisons with the nineteenth century 'must . . . still be left open.' Elsewhere, however, he still posits a golden age, and, in comparison with the earlier period describes how the labouring poor of the Industrial Revolution felt an 'unquantifiable and spiritual sense of loss', and how 'the self-confident, coherent, educated and cultured pre-industrial mechanics and domestic workers' declined and fell (in spite of agreeing also with Engels that the pre-industrial workers lived in 'ignorance and stagnation'). But the researches of Mrs M. D. George, Miss D. Marshall and the Webbs reveal a pre-industrial society that was static and sordid, with the labouring poor on subsistence wages and periodically decimated by cycles, plagues and famines. What Dr Hobsbawm has to prove is that living conditions in the eighteenth century were *better* than in the early nineteenth, not, as we all know, that conditions during the Industrial Revolution were bad . . . .

This debate on the dynamics of social change cannot be concluded here, but some specific social gains of this period might be mentioned to offset in the minds of more impressionable readers the pessimism of Dr Hobsbawm: (i) the increasing social and economic independence of women, (ii) the reduction in child labour, (iii) the growth of friendly societies, trade unions, savings banks, mechanics' institutes and co-operative societies, (iv) the growth of literacy (more of the population could read and write in 1850 than in 1800), and (v) the changing character of social disorder, which, as F. C. Mather recently demonstrated, was much less brutish and destructive in the 1840s than in the 1780s. The Marxist doctrine of social and economic evolution cannot be protected for ever, even by Dr Hobsbawm, from that misfortune, long ago foreseen by Herbert Spencer, of being 'a deduction killed by a fact'. And in this case, the facts are legion.

R. M. Hartwell, 'The Standard of Living during the Industrial Revolution: A Discussion', *Economic History Review*, Vol 16, August 1963, pp 135–46

Questions

a According to Hartwell what contradictions does Hobsbawm make in his argument (lines 1–9)?

b What has reliable historical research shown about pre-industrial society (lines 9–13)?

c What does Hartwell state that the pessimists have to prove (lines 13–15)?

d On what points does Hartwell base his optimistic view (lines 19–29)?

e Explain what 'mechanics' institutes' were (line 21).

* *f* Considering the five criteria used by Hartwell, how strong is the case for the optimists?

8 Real Wages?

How was it – if 1820 to 1850 showed an appreciable rise in the standard-of-living – that after thirty more years of unquestioned improvement between 1850 and 1880 – the unskilled workers of England still lived in the conditions of extreme deprivation revealed, in the 1890s, by Booth and Rowntree?

The first half of the nineteenth century must be seen as a period of chronic under-employment, in which the skilled trades are like islands threatened on every side by technological innovation and by the inrush of unskilled or juvenile labour. Skilled wages themselves often conceal a number of enforced outpayments: rent of machinery, payment for the use of motive power, fines for faulty work or indiscipline, or compulsory deductions of other kinds. Sub-contracting was predominant in the mining, iron and pottery industries, and fairly widespread in building,

whereby the 'butty' or 'ganger' would himself employ less skilled
labourers; while children – piecers in the mills or hurryers in the pits –
were customarily employed by the spinner or the collier. The
Manchester cotton-spinners claimed in 1818, that a wage of £2 3s. 4d.
was subject to the following outpayments:

1st piecer per week	o	9	2
2nd piecer per week	o	7	2
3rd piecer per week	o	5	4
Candles on the average winter and summer per			
week	o	1	6
Sick and other incidental expenses	o	1	6
Expense £1	5	o	[sic]

leaving a balance of 18s. 4d.
In every industry similar cases can be cited, whereby the wages quoted by
workers reveal a different complexion from those by employers.

E. P. Thompson, *The Making of the English Working Class*, 1966,
pp 269–70

Questions

a How does Thompson use evidence of a later period to question the
optimists (lines 1–5)?

b How secure does Thompson think skilled tradesmen were in the early
nineteenth century (lines 6–9)?

c Why does Thompson distrust the wages figures (lines 9–28)?

d Explain the term 'piecer' (line 15).

e How might the system of subcontracting further reduce wages (lines
12–16)?

*   f What are the drawbacks to the kind of evidence Thompson is using in
this extract?

9   Wage Variations

A survey of wages throughout the United Kingdom in 1810 and later
years reveals some large regional variations, with wages in Glasgow
usually, though not invariably, from 1s. to 5s. lower than those paid in
Manchester or Bolton. At the very top of the scale, inevitably, were the
compositors on London morning newspapers, earning £2 8s. a week, an
income which many a curate or governess would have envied. At the
very bottom, equally inevitably, were labourers, both urban and rural,
earning in Manchester 15s. a week, in Glasgow 11s., with farm workers
(except in a few particularly ill-paid counties) averaging 13s. a week. In
between came tradesmen of varying degrees of skill: Carpenters: 25s. a
week in Manchester, 18s. in Glasgow; Bricklayers: 22s. 6d. and 17s;
Masons: 22s. and 17s; Tailors: 18s. 6d. in Manchester, and, unusually, 6d.
more in Glasgow; Shoemakers: 16s. and 15s. and – already a special case,

slipping down the earnings table – hand-loom weavers 16s. 3d. in
15 Manchester, 11s. 6d. in Glasgow. Another survey adds additional trades
such as miners, earning in Scotland 5s. a day, and ironmoulders, high up
the table with 31s. a week. The earnings of the 'mule-spinners', using one
of the earliest inventions to transform the cotton industry, Samuel
Crompton's 'mule' which produced a finer and stronger thread than hand
20 spinning, thus making possible the production of high quality muslin, at
25 – 30s. a week, showed clearly enough that machinery was by no means
a threat to the livelihood of those who learned to master it. Engineers, a
trade barely known twenty years earlier, already earned 28s. a week,
another portent of changes still to come. With the exception of the hand-
25 loom weavers, most of these rates of pay altered little during the
following twenty years, apart from minor variations due to the state of
trade. The pattern of occupations however, changed markedly during
this period. The cotton industry, with only 162 000 employees in 1787
was by 1831 one of the two or three largest in the country, with 833 000.

N. Longmate, *Milestones in Working Class History*, 1975, p 25

Questions

a What did the term 'engineer' mean in 1831 (line 22)?
b What important point about general wage levels does Longmate
highlight?
c What picture of labour in the UK does Longmate's investigation
present?
d If wage levels remained more or less the same until the 1830s, what do
you need to know to form a valid opinion about the standard of
living?
e What two important qualifying factors does Longmate produce at
the end of the extract (lines 27–9)?
* f Using documents 3, 4, 5, 8 and 9 as a basis, on what did a person's
standard of living depend between 1800–50?

10 Are Conclusions Possible?

Can one hope to draw conclusions about the changes in the standard of
living between 1790 and 1850? There is no agreement now; there has
been no agreement by contemporaries arguing ever since those days.
Both sides agree that after 1850 the national income was expanding so fast
5 that, even with wider gaps between rich and poor probably developing,
the poor were benefiting from the expanding economy and industrialisation – again in those things that could be measured.

The lack of a consensus means that one cannot yet speak with
confidence of a single entity, 'the national economy', as far as the standard
10 of living is concerned. The question is whether the hand-loom weaver
was more representative than the adult in the factories who maintained

wages in the face of falling prices. Is the bad year 1842 more typical than the good year of 1845? A lot of evidence, favourable and unfavourable, depends on these two questions: which sector of the economy does it
15 apply to, and to which particular year? . . .

But continuing debate today means that probably no marked general change took place, certainly no *general* movement towards deterioration, such as occurred between 1795 and 1815 from war inflation and high food prices and a shift in distribution of income away from wage earners.
20 This absence of drama in turn may be considered very dramatic given the increase in the population that had to be supported – from under 9 million to over 14 million in those 60 years after 1790 . . . .

P. Mathias, *The First Industrial Nation: Economic History of Britain 1700 – 1914*, 1969, pp 222 – 3

Questions

a On what do optimists and pessimists agree (lines 4 – 7)?

b What crucial piece of evidence does Mathias say is missing (lines 8 – 9)?

c On what basis can a historian confidently make statements about the standard of living (lines 13 – 15)?

* *d* How far do you agree with the conclusion in the final paragraph that there was no marked general change in living standards?

Further reading

R. M. Hartwell (ed.), *The Industrial Revolution* (1967); E. J. Hobsbawm, *Industry and Empire* (1970); P. Mathias, *The First Industrial Nation* (1969); E. P. Thompson, *The Making of the English Working Class* (1966); M. W. Flinn, 'Trends in Real Wages 1750 – 1850', *English Historical Review*, Vol XXVII, Aug. 1974, pp 395 – 413.

II Were the Working Classes Revolutionary?

Introduction

At the close of the Napoleonic Wars, Britain experienced chronic price rises and periods of desperate unemployment. It is the latter factor which appeared to be the catalyst in the periods of political upheaval but when relative stability returned agitation turned to demanding better conditions and wages.

The ways in which workers attempted to organise in order to improve or at least maintain their position varied in four discernable ways:

1 The growth of 'self-help' groups or Friendly Societies to ameliorate the vicissitudes of life by financial contributions.

2 An organised attempt to deal with employers by negotiation or strikes to improve wages and/or conditions.

3 When 2 failed, to take the initiative by rioting or destroying machinery – 'collective bargaining by riot' as Hobsbawm puts it.

4 Political activity such as Chartism. Although Chartism was the single most important working class political movement in Britain in the first half of the nineteenth century, the Charter papered over many cracks. Its lack of unity was a result of its diverse elements. One of the most acute divisions within the movement was whether to employ moral force or physical force to achieve the Charter. But as F. C. Mather points out, 'What existed was not two schools, but a range of opinions which shaded into one another, and individual Chartists often shifted the emphasis in their views so markedly as to give the impression of having changed sides.'

Whenever action, particularly 3 and 4, by lower orders appeared to threaten the concept of a stable society, such phenomena were viewed with grave suspicion by elements of the upper classes.

Did these movements constitute a revolutionary threat, at any time during the first half of the nineteenth century? Certainly, there existed a great fear that English Jacobins would imitate the French Revolution and violently overthrow the existing political system. Some historians claim that such English Jacobins existed as a real threat. Notable amongst the claimants is E. P. Thompson, in *The Making of the English Working Class*, who passionately asserts that between 1790 and 1832, Britain came close to revolution, 1848 being the final echo.

Yet no revolution occurred. If the fuse had been primed, what prevented ignition? In the main, the working class leaders aimed at reform, to bring the government into disrepute, or in extremity to bypass the capitalist system by co-operatives. Weakness and division characterised the movements which frequently displayed a lack of ability or will. It may be more appropriate to ask whether it was the over-reaction of the ruling class which created the spectre of revolution. Indeed the readiness of government agents to believe in the spectre, alongside the existence of a parliamentary secret committee to monitor it, lend credence to this view.

1 The Formation of the Working Class

In the years between 1780 – 1832 most English working people came to feel an identity of interest as between themselves, and as against their rulers and employers. This ruling class was itself much divided, and in fact only gained in cohesion over the same years because certain antagonisms
5 were resolved (or faded into relative insignificance) in the face of an insurgent working class. Thus the working class presence was, in 1832, the most significant factor in British political life. . . . (p 12)
 . . . one direction of the great agitations of the artisans and outworkers, continued over fifty years, was to resist being turned into a proletariat.
10 When they knew that this cause was lost, yet they reached out again, in the Thirties and Forties, and sought to achieve new and only imagined forms of social control. During all this time they were, as a class, repressed and segregated in their own communities. But what the counter-revolution sought to repress grew only more determined in the quasi-
15 legal institutions of the underground. . . . Segregated in this way, their institutions acquired a peculiar toughness and resilience. Class also acquired a peculiar resonance in English life: everything, from their schools to their shops, their chapels to their amusements, was turned into a battleground of class. (p 914)—They fought, not the machine,
20 but the exploitive and oppressive relationships intrinsic to individual capitalism (p 915)
 E. P. Thompson, *The Making of the English Working Class*, 1966, (Pagination of Penguin edition)

Questions

a On which political/economic theorist does Thompson appear to base his views of historical change (lines 8 – 21)? How may this attitude colour his judgement?

b What do you think is meant by the 'quasi-legal institutions of the underground' (lines 14 – 15)?

c In Thompson's opinion how was the working class formed (lines 1 – 3 and lines 16 – 19)?

d In what ways was the ruling class divided (lines 3–6)?

e In what sense can working class agitation be described as regressive or progressive (lines 8–10)?

* *f* Do you consider working class diversities to be so great that it would be more appropriate to talk of working classes rather than working class? Can the ruling class be distinguished as an entity?

* *g* Is class a static or a dynamic historical concept? What are the implications of such a statement?

2 Criticism of the Idea of a Working Class

. . . Thompson's use of evidence to establish conclusions is often faulty, providing a maximum of feeling and a minimum of analysis. In the first place Mr Thompson is ambiguous about statistics. He rejects the method of drawing inferences from statistical data and he attacks those who do so
5 as 'empirical economic historians'. . . . Often Mr Thompson seems to reject quantification as spurious historical method; often he uses it generously to bolster his own arguments. . . . Mr Thompson also tends to use his imagination and some evidence to state what might have happened, and then to proceed as though what might have happened had
10 happened . . . . Phrases such as 'It is equally possible', 'There is no inherent probability', 'There may have been', 'It is not impossible', and 'The true story may be' are common. . . . Mr Thompson's ability to reconstruct history is made easier by commitment to a particular view of society and by the use of Marxist and Hegelian concepts. He is quite clear what would
15 have been good for England and what should have happened; his great problem is to explain why it did not occur . . . the historical pheno- menon of class in Mr Thompson's book remains elusive. He objects to the search of a 'pure specimen' of class, but in dealing with the fact that 'class is a relationship' and that 'class happens' he proceeds to use the term in so
20 many ways that it is difficult to make sense of his definitions, historical analysis or chronology. . . .

> R. M. Hartwell and R. Currie, 'The Making of the English Working Class?', *Economic History Review*, Vol 18, No. 3

Questions

a In the view of Hartwell and Currie what basic assumption has Thompson made which limits his historical judgement (lines 12–14)?

b According to the article, what contradictions exist in Thompson's work (lines 3–12)?

c Where does Thompson draw a false conclusion based on a false premise (lines 7–12)?

d How does Thompson evade defining 'class' (lines 17–21)?

* *e* What are the difficulties in obtaining evidence to demonstrate the existence of revolutionary committees?

3 Fear of Revolution: contemporary accounts for and against Reform Societies

Lord Loughborough to Henry Dundas (Home Secretary) 24th April 1792

Two very intelligent persons with whom I could converse in perfect confidence, ascribe the growth of the Sheffield Club to the disorderly habits of the place, the source of which is in its constitution. The staple manufactory of Cutleryware is under the restraint of a very strict
5 Corporation. The work is carried on by Apprentices and Journeymen who can earn a full maintenance without employing their whole time, and have no inducement to do more, because they do not work for their own account. None of the masters are engaged in this club which they would suppress if they durst. . . . It is very certain that this Sheffield Club
10 was formed by Payne while he was in that neighbourhood, having picked up two or three men of very low condition, but of quicker parts than their companions, who by haranguing at Alehouses, were at last encouraged to become the orators of a Club, very few of whom can write their own names.
Scottish Record Office, *Melville Castle MSS.*, GD 51/1/17/2

Report of Acquaintances to Samuel Shore (A Property Owner in Yorkshire and Derbyshire), Forwarded to The Reverend Christopher Wyvill, May 1792

15 The Society first originated with four or five persons, Mechanics, without having the business in the least suggested them by anyone. The leading people in it are considered in general as persons of good character. . . .
A Parliamentary Reform is their professed object, and the Friends of Liberty believe they keep this object in view; though timid persons, and
20 those who are alarmed at the mention of a Reform, ascribe widely different motives to them, and assert that they aim at nothing but confusion and disorder. The writer of this has frequently conversed with some of the leading members, whom he has found men of understanding, with their minds open to information. Upon questioning them with
25 respect to their views, they have always declared, that all they wished was to spread information amongst the lower classes of people, and to convince them of the existence of abuses, in order that they might join, whenever persons of consequence should think it expedient to come forward, by Petition, or any other legal peaceable way, to obtain a
30 Reform of Parliament.
Quoted in Reverend C. Wyvill (ed.), *Political Papers*, Vol V

Questions

a Why has Lord Loughborough written to Henry Dundas (heading)?
b In what ways do the letters differ in respect of:
   i) information received about the club (lines 1 – 3 and lines 22 – 4)?

ii) the origins of the club (lines 9–14 and lines 15–17)?
iii) the character of the members (lines 10–14 and lines 16–17)?
iv) the aims of the club (lines 9–10 and 18–22)?

c Is there any significance in the formation of working men's political clubs in 1792?

* d What other types of clubs and societies existed? Could they be described as Jacobin?

* e Why was Thomas Paine regarded as the arch-conspirator of revolution?

4 The Luddites. Were they Revolutionaries?

If . . . you were taking the larger view, and looking for a larger purpose, you would need your Luddites to have aims that extended beyond machine breaking and encompassed perhaps some plans to change government and society as a whole. And to achieve such aims you would
5 need to find evidence of organisation beyond that needed to perform the limited local exercises of selective machine breaking. . . . Their (Luddites) political actions are not easy to establish but that does not necessarily mean they did not exist . . . . The expressed fears of revolution seem to me to be more understandable in the context of 1812, but they
10 tell us what people were afraid of, not what was happening. The testimony is rarely first hand and where it comes from those supposed to be implicated themselves, they are supplying information for profit or for saving their skins. The arms stores, the Jacobin cells, the armies, were never found, perhaps because they never existed. The rumour, the gossip,
15 the imagination and exaggeration of the panic stricken and over-zealous, all these rather than the actual state of affairs, were perhaps the origin of the revolution scare that accompanied machine breaking.

M. I. Thomis, *Luddism and the English Working Class*, Popular Politics – Open University A401 II Units 3–6

Questions

a Does Thomis regard the Luddites as an insurrectionary movement (lines 13–14)?

b What evidence would be needed to prove that the Luddites were an insurrectionary movement (lines 2–6)?

c Why are the 'expressed fears of revolution' understandable (lines 8–10 and lines 14–17)?

d Why is evidence about Luddite activities difficult to obtain (lines 11–14)?

* e What economic factors led to the outbreak of Luddism?

* f What grievances did the Luddites express?

5 Revolution 1812 – contemporary accounts

General Maitland (Prescot) to Richard Ryder (Home Secretary) 23 May 1812 (General Maitland was in charge of military operations against the Luddites)

It gives me great satisfaction on considering the whole of the situation of this District (County of Chester), and after weighing in my mind everything I have heard, and everything that has actually occurred since I came here, to be able to state to you my decided Conviction that those
5 who may be concerned in any real Revolutionary Object, are by no means so considerable in numbers as is generally credited by many; and Believing as I do their numbers to be hitherto small, I am equally convinced their plans and Objects, such as they may be, are Crude and Indigested.
10 I have not a doubt that their great supporter was Fear, the operation of which induced many nominally to join them, who the moment they saw themselves protected against them, deserted their Cause, and though undoubtedly the Present Price of Provision and Labour, must press upon the Lower Orders; I do not believe that Dissatisfaction will get any Head,
15 or that the real mischief will increase to any extent, provided a vigilant eye be kept over them.
    Home Office 40.1, 1812

A Letter from William Chippendale (Captain of the Local Militia in Oldham and a Local Magistrate) to Richard Ryder (Home Secretary) 22 May 1812

. . . Of the disturbances which have taken place in this Country, of the peculiar political character and desperate Cast of those Wretches who have been the Formenters of them and of the Object to which their
20 diabolical Efforts are directed . . . I have lately become acquainted with a Member, and one of no Common Activity, of the Secret Revolutionary committee of Royton, a Place in which every Inhabitant (with the exception of not more than five or six) are the most determined and revolutionary Jacobins.
25 . . . I have had various interviews with him, in which he expressed strong Contrition for the Participation he has had in exciting the People to these Enormities and I have endeavoured to avail myself of the Disposition he has manifested by inducing him to make a Disclosure of their Proceedings and to give Information as would lead to the detection
30 of their Leading Men and this complete Frustration of their Designs. I regret, however, to say that hitherto I have exerted all my Address in vain . . . . It is under this impression that I have taken liberty to trouble you upon this occasion and to suggest to your Excellency the propriety of trying him with a small sum of money by War or Reward or proposing
35 to engage him in a contrived service at certain wages.
    Home Office, 1812

Questions

a Which of these two documents would you regard as the more accurate?

b How do the extracts differ in tone?

c How do the extracts differ in description?

* d From what sources could the committee obtain its information?

* e What agencies existed to enforce public order in early nineteenth-century England? How effective were they?

6 Report of the Secret Committee of the House of Commons on the Disturbed State of the Country, 19th February 1817

It appears to your Committee . . . that attempts have been made in various parts of the country as well as in the metropolis to take advantage of the distress in which the labouring and manufacturing classes of the community are at present involved, to induce them to look for
5 immediate relief, not only in a reform of Parliament on the plan of universal suffrage and annual election, but in a total overthrow of all existing establishments and in a division of the landed (property) and extinction of the funded property of the country.

It has been proved that some members of these Societies endeavoured
10 to prepare the means of raising an insurrection. . . . The design was by a sudden rising in the dead of night . . . to surprise and overpower the soldiers in their different barracks, which were to be set on fire . . . a machine was projected for clearing the streets of cavalry. A drawing of this machine fully authenticated and also a manuscript sketch or plan of
15 various important parts of the Tower, found with the drawing of the machine, have been laid before your Committee.

Aspinall and Smith, *English Historical Documents*, Vol XI, 1783–1832, pp 325–9

Questions

a According to the committee what had been the result of working class distress (lines 4–8)?

b Which of the demands particularly threatens vested parliamentary interests (lines 6–8)?

c How was insurrection to be achieved (lines 10–13)?

d Where would the committee obtain its information?

* e How realistic were the conclusions of the committee?

7 The Peterloo Massacre

A little before noon on the 16th August, a body of reformers began to arrive on the scene of action, which was a piece of ground called St.

Peter's Field, adjoining a church of that name in the town of Manchester. These persons bore two banners, surmounted with caps of liberty and bearing the inscription: 'No Corn Laws', 'Annual Parliament', 'Universal Suffrage', 'Vote by Ballot'. Some of these flags after being paraded around the field, were planted in the cart on which the speakers stood; but others remained in different parts of the crowd. Numerous large bodies of reformers continued to arrive from the towns in the neighbourhood of Manchester till about one o'clock, all preceded by flags, and many of them in regular marching order, five deep. Two clubs of female reformers advanced, one of them numbering more than 150 members, and bearing a white silk banner. One body of reformers timed their steps to the sound of a bugle with much of a disciplined air. A band of special constables assumed a position on the field without resistance. The congregated multitude now amounted to a number roundly computed at 80 000, and the arrival of the hero of the day was impatiently expected. At length, Mr Hunt made his appearance, and after a rapturous greeting, was invited to preside; he signified his assent, and mounting a scaffolding began to harangue his admirers. He had not proceeded far when the appearance of the yeomanry cavalry advancing towards the area in a brisk trot, excited a panic in the outskirts of the meeting. They entered the enclosure and after pausing a moment to recover their disordered ranks, and breathe their horses, they drew their swords, and brandished them fiercely in the air. The multitude, by the direction of their leaders, gave three cheers to show that they were undaunted by the intrusion, and the orator had just resumed his speech to assure the people that this was only a trick to disturb the meeting, and to exhort them to stand firm, when the cavalry dashed into the crowd, making for the cart on which the speakers were placed. The multitude offered no resistance, they fell back on all sides. The commanding officer, then approaching Mr Hunt, and brandishing his sword, told him that he was his prisoner. Mr Hunt after enjoining the people to tranquillity, said that he would readily surrender to any civil officer on showing his warrant, and Mr Nadin, the principal police officer, received him in charge. Another person, named Johnson, was likewise apprehended, and a few of the mob; some others against who there were warrants escaped in the crowd. A cry now arose among the military of 'Have at their flags', and they dashed down not only those in the cart, but the others dispersed in the field; cutting to right and left to get at them. The people began running in all directions; and from this moment the yeomanry lost all command of temper; numbers were trampled under the feet of men and horses; many, both men and women, were cut down by sabres; several, and a peace officer in the number, slain on the spot. The whole number of persons injured amounted to between three and four hundred. The populace threw a few stones and brick-bats in their retreat; but in less than ten minutes the ground was entirely cleared of its former occupants, and filled by various bodies of military, both on horse and foot. Mr Hunt was led to prison, not without incurring considerable danger and some injury on his way from

the swords of yeomanry and the bludgeons of police officers; the broken
staves of two of his banners were carried in mock procession before him.
The magistrates directed him to be locked up in a solitary cell, and the
other prisoners were confined with the same precaution.

The town was brought into a tolerably quiet state before night,
military patrols being stationed at the end of almost every street.

Annual Register, 1819

Questions

a What were 'caps of liberty' (line 4)?
b Can the crowd at Peterloo be described as revolutionary (lines 5—6)?
c What impressions of disciplined organisation were given by the
   assembled crowd (lines 10—11)?
d How was the crowd broken up (lines 20—32)?
e Who appears to have been responsible for the disorder (lines 36—44)?
* f What other interpretations have been made of the incident at St.
   Peter's Field?
* g What is the historical significance of Peterloo?

8 Chartism

a) Lovett discusses Physical Force

The whole physical force agitation is harmful and injurious to the
movement. Muskets are not what are wanted, but education and
schooling of the working people. Stephens and O'Connor are shattering
the movement. . . . Violent words do not slay the enemies but the
friends of the movement. O'Connor wants to take everything by storm,
and to pass the Charter into law within a year. All this hurry and haste,
this bluster and menace of armed opposition can only lead to outbreaks
and to the destruction of Chartism.

Quoted in Parliamentary Representation, O.U.P., p 22

b) O'Connor on Physical Force

He [O'Connor] had never counselled the people to use physical force,
because he felt that those who did were fools to their own cause; but, at
the same time, those who decried it preserved their authority by physical
force alone. . . . He counselled them against all rioting, all civil war, but
still, in the hearing of the House of Commons, he would say, that rather
than see the constitution violated, while the people were in daily want, if
no other man would do so, if the constitution was violated, he would himself lead the people to death or glory . . . . His desire was to try moral force
as long as possible, even to the fullest extent, but he would always have
them bear in mind, that it is better to die freemen than to live slaves. Every
conquest which was called honourable had been achieved by physical
force, but they did not want it, because if all hands were pulling for

Universal Suffrage they would soon pull down the stronghold of corruption. He hoped and trusted that out of the exercise of that judgement which belonged exclusively to the working class, a union would arise, and from that union a moral power would be created,
25 sufficient to establish the rights of the poor man; but if this failed, then let every man raise his arm in defence of that which his judgement told him was justice.

R. G. Gammage, *History of the Chartist Movement*, 1854

Questions

a In what ways do Lovett and O'Connor differ in their views on working class tactics (lines 1 – 3 and lines 16 – 22)?

b Under what circumstances does O'Connor advocate the use of force (lines 22 – 25)?

c How does O'Connor justify the use of violence (lines 14 – 16)?

* *d* When Chartists attempted insurrection why did they fail?

* *e* What grievances further to those in the Charter gave Chartists cause for concern?

9   Chartism and Public Order

'How are the people to obtain the Charter, there being a majority of the Commons against it?' This was the problem which permanently taxed the minds of the Chartist leaders and drove some of them to revolution. The Convention of 1839 tried to provide an answer, but its voice was lost
5 in a maelstrom of hesitation and indecision. (p 148) . . . . When several provincial W.M.A.s protested about the frequent references to 'physical force', London Democrats reminded them of the respectability of previous English revolutions and the glory of the French example. The motto of the L.D.A. and the Great Northern Union – 'peaceably if we
10 may, forcibly if we must' – summed up the radical version of history and the Chartist instinct. (p 149) . . . most Chartists regarded arming as a natural form of protection against another Peterloo. Chartists of all descriptions talked much of government plots and the 'violence' of police and civil authorities. The Rural Police Bill, Irish Coercion Acts and the
15 'Gagging Act' of 1848 indicated the willingness of the Whig ministers to invade people's rights. By encouraging the establishment of armed associations in 1839, and by the parallel arrest of prominent Chartists, the government gave some weight to a conspiracy theory. (p 150) . . . . In the event *sui generis* Chartist violence was confined to the years 1839 – 42
20 and 1848. These were the periods of Chartist anguish; of millenial hopes and crushing setbacks. (p 155) . . . .

David Jones, *Chartism and the Chartists*, 1975

Questions

a What tactical problem faced the Chartists when their petitions were rejected (lines 1–3)?

b What prevented the Chartists from taking action (lines 4–5)?

c What does David Jones mean when he writes of the 'Chartist instinct' and the 'radical version of history' (lines 10–11)?

d What was 'the "Gagging Act" of 1848' (line 15)?

e According to David Jones what factors contributed to a 'conspiracy theory' (line 18)?

* f Why was Chartist violence confined to the years 1839–42 and 1848?

10 The Fear of Chartism

It must be remembered that at the time for many people Chartism aroused very real fears. To the middle and upper classes a Chartist rebellion was more than a remote possibility. The Home Office papers contain numerous reports to the Home Secretary from anxious magis-
5 trates and Lord Lieutenants passing on rumours of Chartist insurrections. Some of the reports are well founded, others have much less justification . . . . Certainly it was the fear of mob violence that did much to shape the attitudes of the authorities and of sections of the general public to the grievances of the working classes.
10   Nevertheless, it is important to take into account that, for a variety of reasons, fear was sometimes deliberately fostered by the authorities. There was a tendency to ascribe any industrial unrest or disturbances to the work of the Chartists and the more violent aspects of these disturbances were often emphasised in order to win the support of the
15 uncommitted. By this means the authorities hoped to produce a united opposition against the rioters or strikers which would help prevent the disturbances . . . caused by Chartist agitators, [and] the authorities often succeeded in obscuring the very real grievances of the strikers.

John Golby, 'Chartism and Public Order', *Popular Politics* O.U. A401 11 3–6

Questions

a Why did Chartism arouse 'very real fears' (lines 1–2)?

b How did the authorities express their attitudes towards the grievances of the working classes (lines 6–9)?

c Why did the authorities deliberately foster fear against the Chartists (lines 15–18)?

d What did the authorities hope to achieve by these tactics (lines 14–15)?

* e Could the aims and activities of working class movements and organisations in the first half of the nineteenth century be described as revolutionary?

Further reading

E. P. Thompson, *The Making of the English Working Class* (1966); E. J. Hobsbawm, *The Age of Revolution 1789–1848* (1962); A. Briggs, *The Age of Improvement* (1959); F. C. Mather, *Chartism* (1972); D. Jones, *Chartism and the Chartists* (1975).

III Trade Unions

Introduction

In July 1901 the House of Lords decided that the Taff Vale Railway Company could sue the Amalgamated Society of Railway Servants for damages as compensation for lost income as a result of a strike in August 1900. Which Union could now dare to strike and risk crippling litigation? The Lords' decision provoked a majority of Trade Unions to support the idea of a Labour Party in Parliament and placed in perspective the status gained by Trade Unions in the previous hundred years.

Trade Unions had been a direct result of the Industrial Revolution. As guilds became obsolete and government ceased to regulate wages, skilled tradesmen felt themselves forced to combine to protect their interests. Such combinations were specifically different in intent from the insurance policy of Friendly Societies. Unfortunately, the emergence of such combinations coincided with the French Revolution. Consequently, they forfeited legality at the hands of a sensitive establishment and those who ruled found it difficult to disassociate unions of workmen from the idea of revolution.

It was not until the Royal Commission of 1867 that the respectability of Trade Unions was firmly accepted. They had grown among skilled workers in spite of the repercussions of Luddism, the G.N.C.T.U. failure and Chartism and had a pedigree which preceded the 'New Model' concept of the Webbs. In 1868 the TUC was founded, being formally constituted in 1871. By 1875 they were free from the last trace of criminal law.

In the 1880s and 1890s the consolidation of the unions coincided with financial and industrial crisis. Despite the outspoken opposition of leaders such as Tillett to 'hare-brained chatterers and magpies of Continental revolutionists', fear of Trade Unionism persisted among those who ruled. It was against such a background that the Taff Vale decision was reached, just before *The Times* ran a series of articles on 'The Crisis of British Industry' blaming Trade Unions for the weakness of British industry against its rivals.

1 The Combination Acts

Whereas great numbers of Journeymen Manufacturers and Workmen, in various parts of this Kingdom, have, by unlawful Meetings and Combinations, endeavoured to obtain Advance of their Wages, and to effectuate other Illegal Purposes; and the Laws at present in Force against
5 such unlawful Conduct have been found to be inadequate to the Suppression thereof, whereby it is become necessary that more effectual Provision should be made against such unlawful Combinations . . . be it enacted . . . That . . . all Contracts, Covenants, and Agreements what- soever, in Writing or not in Writing, at any Time or Times heretofore
10 made or entered into by or between any Journeymen Manufacturers or other Workmen, or by persons within this Kingdom, for obtaining an Advance of Wages of them . . . or for lessening or altering their or any of their usual Hours or Times of working, or for decreasing the Quantity of Work, or for preventing or hindering any Person or Persons from
15 employing whomsoever he, she, or they shall think proper to employ in his, her, or their Manufacture . . . .

An Act to Prevent Unlawful Combinations of Workmen, 2nd July 1799

. . . and every journeyman and workman who . . . shall be guilty of any of the said offences, being thereof lawfully convicted, upon his own confession or the oath or oaths of one or more credible witness or
20 witnesses, before any two Justices of the Peace . . . shall, by order of such Justices, be committed to and confined to the Common Gaol . . . , for any time not exceeding three calendar months, or . . . be committed to some house of correction . . . and . . . kept to hard labour for any time not exceeding two calendar months.

Combination Act, 1800

Questions

a Why have the Combination Laws been passed (lines 1 – 5)?
* b Why should the Combination Laws have been passed at this particular time?
c Upon what evidence could a workman be convicted (lines 18 – 20)?
d What penalties could be imposed (lines 21 – 4)?
* e What laws already existed under which workmen could be pro- secuted for restraint of trade?

2 Opposition to the Combination Acts

Now, you will observe Wilberforce, that this punishment is inflicted in order to prevent workmen from uniting together . . . . Every man's labour is his *property* . . . . The cotton spinners had their labour to sell; or at least they thought so . . . . The purchasers were powerful and rich,

5 and wanted them to sell it at what the spinners deemed too low a price. In
order to be a match for the rich purchasers, the sellers of labour agree to
assist one another, and thus to live as well as they can; till they can obtain
what they deem to be a proper price . . . . If men be attacked either in the
market or their shops; if butchers, bakers, farmers, millers be attacked
10 with a view of forcing them to sell their commodities at a price lower
than they demand, the assailants are deemed rioters, and are hanged!
   This Combination Act does, however, say that the 'masters' shall not
combine against the workmen . . . the utmost fine that the two justices
can inflict is a *fine of twenty pounds!* But, and now mark the difference.
15 Mark it, Wilberforce; note it down as a proof of the happiness of your
'free British labourers': mark, that the masters cannot be called upon by
the Justices to *give evidence against themselves or their associates.*

W. Cobbett, *Political Register*, August 30th, 1823

Questions

a How does Cobbett argue that the Combination Laws are illogical and
unfair?
* b How do you account for the apparent contradiction in Wilberforce as
an anti-slaver and favourer of Combination Laws? Explain what
Cobbett means by the phrase 'Every man's labour is his *property*' (lines
2−3).
c What would be the difficulty in proving a combination of employers
(lines 16−17)?
* d Who was Cobbett and what view of society did he hold?

3 Report of Select Committee advocating the repeal of the Combination Acts

On Combination Laws

. . . it appears, by the evidence before the Committee . . . *That* the laws
have not only not been efficient to prevent Combinations, either of
masters or workmen; but on the contrary, have, in the opinion of many
of both parties, had a tendency, to produce mutual irritation and distrust,
5 and to give a violent character to the Combinations, and to render them
highly dangerous to the peace of the community.
   That it is the opinion of this Committee, that masters and workmen
should be freed from these restrictions, as regards the rate of wages and
the hours of working, and be left at perfect liberty to make such
10 arrangements as that they mutually think proper.
   That it is absolutely necessary, when repealing the Combination Laws, to
enact such a law as may efficiently, and by summary process punish either
workmen or masters, who by threats, intimidation, or act of violence,
should interfere with the perfect freedom which ought to be allowed to

15   each party, of employing his labour or capital in the manner he may deem
most advantageous.
The Report of the Select Committee on Artisans and Machinery, 1824

Questions

a Why does the Select Committee wish to see an end to the
Combination Laws (lines 1 − 6)?
* *b* What evidence could be cited to support the view that 'a violent
character' was given to the combinations?
c What advantages or disadvantages would accrue from free
bargaining?
d What restriction had been placed on combinations of workmen?
e How could the final section of the Report be used against workmen in
pursuit of trade union activities?
* *f* Why would the argument against the Combination Laws be likely to
be successful by 1824?

4 Francis Place collecting evidence against the Combination Acts

The delegates from the working people had reference to me . . . I
examined and cross-examined them; took down the leading particulars of
each case, and then arranged the matter as briefs for Mr Hume, and, as a
rule, for the guidance of the witnesses, a copy was given to each . . . thus
5   he was enabled to go on with considerable ease, and to anticipate or rebut
objections . . . . They (the workmen) were filled with false notions, all
attributing their distresses to wrong causes, which I, in this state of the
business, dared not attempt to remove. Taxes, machinery, laws against
combination, the will of the masters, the conduct of magistrates, these
10   were the fundamental causes of all their sorrows and privations. All
expected a great and sudden rise of wages, when the Combination Laws
should be repealed; not one of them had any idea of the connection
between wages and population. I had to discuss everything with them
most carefully, to arrange and prepare everything, and so completely did
15   these things occupy my time, that for more than these three months I had
hardly time for rest.
Francis Place, *The Place Mss.* 27,798ff. pp 20 − 4

Questions

a How carefully did Hume and Place prepare their ground against the
Combination Laws (lines 1 − 3)?
b What reasons did the interviewed workmen advance for their distress
(lines 8 − 9)?
* *c* How would the workmen, untutored, have harmed the anti-
combination law lobby?

*
   d What did Place mean when he wrote, 'not one of them had any idea of the connection between wages and population' (lines 12−13)?

   e How did Hume and Place manage to get the Combination Laws repealed? What was the consequence of repeal and how did government react to it?

5 Aims of the G.N.C.T.U.

The members of this Union have discovered that competition in the sale of their productions is the chief and immediate cause of their poverty and degradation, and that they can never overcome either as long as they shall conduct their affairs individually, and in opposition to each other.

5   They are, therefore, about to form national companies of production; each trade or manufacture to constitute one grand company or association, comprising all the individuals in the business throughout Great Britain and Ireland; but each trade and manufacture to be united to all others by a general bond of interest by which they will exchange their
10 productions with each other upon the principle of equitable exchange of labour for a fair equal value of labour; and all articles, upon a principle of economy and general advantage will be produced, of the best quality only.

   The next step in gradation will be the union of master traders and
15 manufacturers with the operatives and manual producers; and when these two parties shall fully understand the value of this union, the Government will not only feel the necessity of uniting with them, but it will also discover the advantages to the whole empire of this national bond of union.

   From '*The Crisis*', a speech by Robert Owen on the G.N.C.T.U., 19 October, 1833

Questions

   a What purpose was the G.N.C.T.U. to serve (lines 1−4)?

   b On what principle would the exchange of goods be based (lines 9−13)?

   c How would the capitalist system be replaced (lines 14−18)?

   d Was the G.N.C.T.U. atypical of union organisation during the 1830s?

   e What factors contributed to the failure of the G.N.C.T.U.?

6 'New Model' Unions?

The history of trade unionism in the later 1830s and early 1840s has been inadequately investigated, but there is abundant evidence in the Report of the Select Committee on Combinations in 1838, and also in local newspapers and surviving, though scrappy, trade union records, to
5 indicate that a large number of societies remained in existence after 1834.

They had to face great difficulties between 1836 and 1842 because of serious trade depression: the burden of unemployment, wage reductions and loss of membership may have caused some societies to collapse, but most of them appear to have survived. These, of course, were of the sectional, skilled type — unskilled labourers still remained almost entirely unorganised — and there was no change in the character of trade unionism during these years; when trade revived and the forward movement among trade unions was resumed in the 1840s, it was along the old lines.

A. E. Musson, *British Trade Unions 1800—1875*, 1972, pp 34—5

Questions

a How does Musson account for the decline of trade unions in the late 1830s (lines 6—7)? Why should this factor explain trade union decline?

b In the light of what Musson writes, can we continue to speak of a 'New Model' unionism emerging in the 1840s?

c What evidence does Musson quote to support the argument that trade unions continued to operate 'along the old lines' (line 14)?

* d Why should the unskilled remain 'almost entirely unorganised' (lines 10—11)?

* e Did a débâcle occur in the trade union movement after the collapse of the G.N.C.T.U.? What particular incident in 1834 is responsible for such an impression?

* f What are the assumed characteristics of the New Model Unions? Why should they fare so well during the 1850s and 1860s?

7 The Diversity of Working Class Divisions

To sum up. The concept of the labour aristocracy has had its value in drawing attention to the differences within the working class; but if it implies the existence in the late nineteenth and early twentieth century of a labour élite distinctly separated from lower strata and marked by political behaviour of an acquiescent type, then it is a concept that does more harm than good to historical truth. To be sure, in some industries the craftsmen did manage to perpetuate, sometimes even to extend, a tight control over entry into their trades. But the number of industries in which this was possible was constantly in decline after the onset of the industrial revolution. The growth of the factory and mining population in the nineteenth century meant the growth of a more homogeneous working class than had existed previously, and in this working class there was no aristocracy, unless we think of foremen, who, although they often appeared in wage statistics, did not normally belong to trade unions. As for politics, it is clear that Marxist historians have completely got the wrong end of the stick: militancy was much more likely to be found among the better-off than among the poorer workers. We may notice, as

a pendant to the discussion, that recruitment to the Communist Party,
both in this country and in other countries of Europe, has been much
20 more successful among more highly-paid manual workers than among
those of lesser income. Thus we can agree after all with Professor Hugh
Seton-Watson, who has examined this problem in an international context, that in its political application 'The theory of the labour aristocracy
is as artificial as the theory of the class struggle within the peasantry'.

> H. Pelling, *Popular Politics and Society in Late Victorian Britain,*
> 1968, p 61

Questions

a   What do you think is meant by 'political behaviour of an acquiescent
type' (line 5)?

b   What fundamental objection does Pelling have to the concept of a
'labour aristocracy' (lines 5—6)?

c   What evidence does Pelling put forward to suggest that the skilled
craftsmen were not acquiescent (lines 16—25)?

d   Why should Marxist historians claim that the labour élite accommodated themselves to capitalism?

e   Why should skilled workers restrict entry into their trades (lines 6—
8)?

*   f   In the light of this extract, what comments could be made in relation
to E. P. Thompson's postulation of a working class unity? (see II *Were
the Working Classes Revolutionary?* p 18)

8   The Royal Commission on Trade Unions 1868—9

It does not appear to be borne out by the evidence that the disposition to
strike on the part of workmen is in itself the creation of unionism, or that
the frequency of strikes increases in proportion to the strength of the
union. It is indeed affirmed by the leaders of unions that the effect of
5 established societies is to diminish the frequency, and certainly the
disorder, of strikes, and to guarantee a regularity of wages and hours
rather than to engage in constant endeavours to improve them
. . . taking the . . . general evidence provided by the return of our export
trade for the last few years, we cannot state that we have traced any
10 distinct connexion between its fluctuation in particular employments and
the prevalence of trades unions in these employments. (*Majority*)
. . . We are of the opinion that no adequate ground has been
shown for the continuance of special laws relating exclusively to the
employment of labour . . . offences described under the general terms
15 'intimidation', 'molestation', and 'obstruction' . . . should be dealt with
under the general criminal law. (*Minority*)

> *Eleventh and Final Report, Royal Commission on Trade Unions,*
> 1868—9

Questions

a Explain in your own words the findings of the Commission.
b What is the purpose of the clause referring to the export trade (lines 8–11)?
c Why has the Minority Report thought it necessary to end the 'special laws relating . . . to the employment of labour' (line 13)?
* d Explain why the Royal Commission on Trade Unions was established.

9 Amending the Conspiracy and Protection of Property Act 1875

3 An agreement or combination by two or more persons to do or procure to be done any act in contemplation of furtherance of a trade dispute between employers and workmen shall not be indictable as a conspiracy if such act committed by one person would not be punishable
5 as a crime.
5 Where any person wilfully and maliciously breaks a contract of service or of hiring, knowing or having reasonable cause to believe that the probable consequence of his so doing, either alone or in combination with others, will be to endanger human life, or cause serious bodily
10 injury, or expose valuable property whether real or personal to destruction or serious injury, he shall on conviction thereof by a court of summary jurisdiction, or on indictment as hereinafter mentioned, be liable either to pay a penalty not exceeding twenty pounds, or be imprisoned for a term not exceeding three months . . . .

An Act to Amend the Law relating to Conspiracy and to the Protection of Property, 13 August, 1875

Questions

a On what legal grounds had Trade Unions been prosecuted before 1875?
b How does clause 5 attempt to define picketing?
c What could Trade Unions now do legitimately?
* d After the passing of the 1870 Trade Union Act how was the law concerning picketing still vague?
* e What other legal difficulties remained in the way of Trade Union activity after 1875?

10 The New Unions

. . . the regeneration of the Trade Union Movement dates from this great social event (Dockers' Strike 1889). Trade Unionism among the general workers . . . was an absolute weakling, regarded as an illegi-

timate offspring, and treated like one by the well established and
5 respectable Trade Unionism of the skilled crafts and trades. To set our
Union on its feet, and to win the respect of the craft Unions we had to
demonstrate the strength of our purpose, the soundness of our strategy,
and the skill of our generalship in actual warfare with the employers. The
Dock Strike was a test, not only of intelligence and will . . . but of the
10 ability to seize opportunities as they arose, to evoke and make use of
public sympathy as one of the weapons of our warfare, and to transform
militant enthusiasm and hectic excitement into Trade Union loyalty and
sober realism . . . .

Ben Tillett, '*Memories and Reflections*' pp 117–120

Questions

a   According to Ben Tillett, what view of unskilled workers did the
    Trade Union Movement have (lines 2–5)?
b   Compare this document with document seven. Does this support or
    refute Pelling's argument?
c   How did the dockers prove themselves to the Trade Union
    Movement and the general public (lines 6–13)?
*
d   What did Tillett mean when he referred to the 'regeneration of the
    Trade Union Movement' (line 1)?
*
e   What was the impact of the organisation of the unskilled on the Trade
    Union Movement?

11   Report of the Royal Commission on Labour 1894

The general impression left by the information before us is that the level
of wage rates has risen considerably during the last fifty years both in
respect of their nominal value and (with the exception of house rents in
large towns) their power of purchasing commodities. At the same time it
5 appears that the daily hours of labour have during the same period been
in most cases shortened, and the sanitary conditions of work have
improved. (*Majority*)

Notwithstanding the great increase in national wealth, whole sections
of the population . . . at least five millions, are unable to obtain a
10 subsistence compatible with health or efficiency.

Probably two millions are every year driven to accept Poor Relief in one
form or another. . . . Even in the well organised skilled trades, where the
normal working day is often nine hours, or less, an excessive amount of
overtime is systematically worked. . . . Many thousands of workers still
15 toil under circumstances which make disease and accident an inevitable
accompaniment of their lives . . . . (*Minority*)

Fifth and Final Report, *Royal Commission on Labour*, 1894

Questions

a   In what respects did the Majority and Minority Reports differ?
b   Why should there be a conflict of views?

c Do the respective views of the Majority and Minority Reports indicate anything about the membership of the Royal Commission?

* *d* What evidence could be cited to support either view?

* *e* Does the Report indicate anything about the strength of the Trade Union Movement?

12 Trade Unions and Politics 1899

Mr Holmes (Cardiff) then moved: 'That this Congress, having regard to its decisions in former years and with a view to securing a better representation of the interests of Labour in the House of Commons, hereby instructs the Parliamentary Committee to invite the co-operation
5 of the Co-operative Societies, Socialistic Societies, Trade Unions, and other working organisations to jointly co-operate on lines mutually agreed upon in convening a Special Congress of representatives of such of the above-named organisations as may be willing to take part to devise ways and means of securing the return of an increased number of Labour
10 members to the next Parliament.'

He said that the sooner Trade Unionists recognised the fact that it was only by dissociating themselves from both the great political parties that they could obtain the balance of power, so that they could dictate their own terms to either Liberals or Conservatives, the better it would be for
15 the interests of Labour. (*Cheers*)

The Congress then divided on the resolution, which was carried amid cheers and counter-cheers by 546 000 votes to 434 000.

Report on the TUC, *Reynold's Newspaper*, 10th September 1899

Questions

a Why has Mr Holmes suggested that Labour should have its own representatives in parliament (lines 11 − 15)?

b What did Holmes mean when he referred to them holding 'the balance of power' (line 13)?

c What advantages would accrue from a united Labour front (lines 2 − 3)?

d Why should so many Trade Unionists not agree with the idea of a united Labour political strategy?

* *e* When had the TUC been formed and why was it reluctant to enter the political arena initially?

13 New Unionism

It was the special characteristics of new unionism that made it the immediate target of ruling class fury. Recent research has modified the picture of new unionism that has been generally accepted, and today it is

recognised that 1889 was less of a break with the past than was formerly
believed. There were stirrings, and organisation, among the unskilled
workers half a dozen years before 1889, and, on the other hand, the old
skilled unions were in some respects less conservative than is usually
believed. Nevertheless, when all the necessary qualifications have been
added to the traditional interpretation of old and new unionism, it is
important not to underestimate the climacteric of 1889. The economic
problems of the unskilled and semi-skilled trade unionists were very
different from those of the skilled workers, and their industrial methods
and tactics were perforce also different. While the old unions were able to
rely upon the skill of their members as a crucial bargaining weapon, the
new unions were at all times, even in the years of good trade, subject to
the pressures of an overstocked labour market. Picketing, for instance,
was rarely a major problem in the strike action of many sections of skilled
workers. The Webbs noted that among the cotton spinners of Lancashire,
or the boilermakers on the north east coast, or the coalminers in well
organised districts, both sides to an industrial dispute knew that when
work was resumed the same men would have to be taken on. The
problem of scab labour did not, therefore, arise in the virulent form that
occurred in the casual and semi-skilled trades. 'Picketing, in fact, is a mark
not of Trade Unionism, but of its imperfection.' So the Webbs wrote in
1896. The position was very different, for example, in the ports
employing dock labour, where only a proportion of those applying for
work on any one day would be accepted and where much of the work
could be performed by agricultural labour or casual labour drafted in
from outside. In such circumstances, and these were familiar in many
other industries, it was immensely more difficult to make a strike solid or
to achieve stable unions. Outside the highly skilled trades, to win even an
approximation to the closed shop or to ensure that blackleg labour did
not swamp a strike, militant tactics were demanded which the older
unionists had pioneered decades before but which, by the end of the
1880s, they believed they no longer needed. The employers, too, in the
semi-and unskilled trades were more uncompromising than their fellows
in industries where unionism had long been established; and their first,
and for men of property not unnatural, reaction was to smash these new
upstart organisations rather than attempt to meet them on common
ground.

J. Saville, 'Trade Unions and Free Labour: The Background to
the Taff Vale Decision' from *Essays in Labour History 1886–1926*,
ed. A. Briggs and J. Saville, 1971, pp 317–50

Questions

a According to Saville, why was new unionism in 1889 not a new
phenomenon (lines 5–8)?

b What were the particular problems of the unskilled workers as
opposed to skilled (lines 10–16)?

c Why did the unskilled workers have to be more militant than the skilled workers (lines 16–29)?

d Why did employers particularly resent the emergence of unskilled unions (lines 29–35)?

e Can you reconcile document 7 with document 13?

* *f* By 1900 how far had the Trade Union Movement come to reflect the structure of the working classes and to represent their interests?

Further reading

H. Pelling, *A History of British Trade Unionism* (1968); A. E. Musson, *British Trade Unions 1800–1875* (1972); A. Briggs & J. Saville (eds), *Essays in Labour History* (1971); S. & B. Webb, *The History of Trade Unionism* (1920).

IV   Laissez-Faire and State Intervention: The Economy

Introduction

The term laissez-faire has traditionally been used to describe the state's reluctance to interfere in industrial and social activity. Bentham, J. S. Mill and Smiles emphasised government's role to be to rule rather than legislate, but the first broadside to mercantilism was delivered by Adam Smith in his work 'An Inquiry into the Nature and Causes of the Wealth of Nations'.

The Napoleonic Wars hindered positive action on Smith's initiative, while the vested interests of landowners were protected after 1815 by the Corn Laws. These became the symbolic citadel which free traders proceeded to storm. The repeal of the Corn Laws had wider implications than the battle for free trade but was seen by free traders as the dawn of a new era for the leading industrial nation, as the benefits of an expanding economy, facilitated by limited liability legislation, percolated to every stratum of society.

Free trade served Britain well as long as prosperity and, therefore, the scope of the individual entrepreneur grew. However, as foreign competition began to match, and even overhaul, British industry in the final decades of the century the philosophy came under attack from a growing lobby for protectionism, led by Joseph Chamberlain. In the atmosphere of the New Imperialism he advocated an imperial association in which free trade could carry on, but protected by tariffs against extra-imperial rivals. Thus, by the turn of the century, the free trade v. protection controversy stood unresolved.

It was in the field of economics that the concept of laissez-faire was most obviously at work. Some historians have questioned the appropriateness of applying the term to the nineteenth century. George Kitson Clark has labelled it 'an encouragement to error'.[1] It is probably when applied to social legislation where various stimuli prodded government to respond pragmatically to novel problems, that the philosophy of laissez-faire was weakest.

---

1   G. Kitson Clark, *An Expanding Society: Britain 1830–1900* (1967) p 162

1 The Favouring and Resisting Forces

As to the former, [forces promoting the extension of State power] pride of place must of course be given to the changes in size, distribution and economic functions of the population occasioned by the agrarian changes of the eighteenth and nineteenth centuries. . . . The wages contract was
5 substituted for more complex and intra-personal relationships; and as the town became more densely packed there was progressive deterioration in living and sanitary standards, further hastened by the presence of manufacture with its smoke, dirt, trade refuse and polluted water . . . it was these which set the problem for which more collectivized and more
10 centralised social organisation and state regulation had ultimately to provide the answers. They furnished the raw material, the opportunity and the stimulus for radical, tory and humanitarian collectivists alike, at any rate for those whose actions led inexorably towards collectivism, however little they appreciated or intended this themselves . . . the social
15 upheavals which set the problems also ultimately helped to produce the answers. It may perhaps be clearest to divide this aspect of the matter into three. . . .

. . . there had come into being bodies of professionals who were beginning to apply the correct method of investigation and who were
20 convinced from their earlier successes that for almost every problem there was a solution which experiment sooner or later would reveal. Thus in every technical difficulty the administration had men to turn to; for every technical measure of regulation and control they had men to call on to enforce it.

25 It also had a system of communications which made centralisation practicable; and both large scale and specialised industries which could produce the tools for social amelioration rapidly in large quantities and . . . cheaply.

The second assisting force I have called political . . . . The Reform
30 Act of 1832 shifted the balance of power in society . . . . The older notions that the business of government was essentially executive . . . were dying. . . . In a word legislation became both the business of the ministry, and systematic and continuous.

The third major factor . . . was humanitarianism . . . In a variety of
35 ways the general revival in religion and piety . . . promoted new social attitudes. For example one of its fruits was a novel and intense concern for sexual morality and 'decent' standards of behaviour.

As to Benthamism . . . first it was a programme for reforming laws by applying the devastating test of utility to every branch of government.
40 Secondly it was extraordinarily inventive in devising universal administrative schemes to replace the existing inefficiencies. Lastly it depended on men behaving rationally.

. . . In short the age in which we speak, c. 1830−70, was one of positive and aggressive individualism; and if during this period the foundations of
45 the modern state were laid, it only happened because of the immense

pressure from beneath of the promoting factors, only because of the great difficulty of measuring particular actions against the uncertain yardstick of individualism, and only because a large number of measures . . . slipped through unnoticed.

50 . . . Collectivism was never a doctrine in nineteenth-century England, never formulated by a thinker of commanding ability, never applied deliberately and consciously to law.

. . . during the middle period [1840–1870] the survival of the local tradition of government and a vast range of local vested interests, new
55 and old, did much to halt a vital movement towards centralization at a decisive stage.

. . . Equally the opponents of Toryism provided a block to centralization and collectivism. During their struggle for political power those of them who were clients and beneficiaries of the industrial revolution had
60 come to adopt an extreme, often fundamentalist, form of *laissez-faire*. Competition, individual self-interest and the profit motive were to be given an open field for action as was compatible with indispensable social bonds.

O. MacDonagh, *Early Victorian Government 1830–1870*, 1977, pp 1–21

Questions

a What were the preconditions favouring the extension of state control and regulation (lines 1–8)?

b Was the extension of state control intended by those who advocated legislation (lines 11–14)?

c In what way did the social upheavals of this period provide the basis for solutions to their problems (lines 18–28)?

d How did the older notions of the functions of government begin to die out (lines 29–33)?

e What intellectual and religious movements provided the stimuli for state action?

f What forces were opposed to the extension of state control?

* g What examples of state interference prior to the nineteenth century were there in the economic life of the country?

2 An Inquiry into the Nature and Causes of the Wealth of Nations

That security which the laws in Great Britain give to every man that he shall enjoy the fruits of his own labour, is alone sufficient to make any country flourish, notwithstanding these and twenty other absurd regulations of commerce . . . . The natural effort of every individual to
5 better his own condition, when suffered to extend itself with freedom and security, is so powerful a principle, that it is alone, and without any

assistance, not only capable of carrying on the society to wealth and prosperity, but of surmounting a hundred impertinent obstructions which the folly of human laws too often incumbers its operations; . . . (p 540)

Were all nations to follow the liberal system of free exportation and free importation, the different states into which a great continent was divided would so far resemble the different provinces of a great empire . . . . (p 538)

Nothing, however, can be more absurd than this whole doctrine of the balance of trade . . . . When two places trade with one another, this doctrine supposes that, if the balance be even, neither of them loses or gains . . . . Both suppositions are false. A trade which is forced by means of bounties and monopolies, may be, and commonly is disadvantageous to the country in whose favour it is meant to be established, . . . But that trade which, without force or constraint, is naturally and regularly carried on between any two places, is always advantageous, though not always equally so, to both. By advantage or gain, I understand, not the increase of the quantity of gold and silver, but that of the exchangeable value of the annual produce of the land and labour of the country, or the increase of the annual revenue of its inhabitants. (pp 488–9)

A. Smith, *An Inquiry into the Nature and Causes of the Wealth of Nations*, 1976 edn

Questions

a   According to Adam Smith, what was the basis of Britain's prosperity (lines 1–10)?
b   Why do trade regulations obstruct the achievement of prosperity (lines 4–10)?
c   How would the adoption of free trade promote world peace and stability (lines 11–14)?
d   Why is the concept of a balance of trade a fallacy (lines 15–23)?
* e   What economic system is Adam Smith criticising in the last part of the extract (lines 23–6)?

3   Introduction to the Principles of Morals and Legislation

. . . By the principle of utility is meant that principle which approves or disapproves of every action whatsoever, according to the tendency which it appears to have to augment or diminish the happiness of the party whose interest is in question . . . I say of every action whatsoever, and therefore not only of every action of a private individual, but of every measure of government.

. . . It is vain to talk of the interest of the community, without understanding what is in the interest of the individual. A thing is said to pro-

mote the interest, or to be *for* the interest, of an individual, when it tends
10   to add to the sum total of his pleasures: or, what comes to the same thing,
to diminish the sum total of his pains.

. . . A measure of government (which is but a particular kind of action,
performed by a particular person or persons) may be said to be
comfortable or dictated by the principle of utility, when in like manner
15   the tendency which it has to augment the happiness of the community is
greater than any which it has to diminish it.

> J. Bentham, *The Works of Jeremy Bentham*, Vol I, 1843, first
> published 1789

Questions

a According to Bentham, what should be the basis of government
   legislation (lines 1–6)?
b Why is it 'vain to talk of the interest of the community' (lines 7–11)?
c What should be the criteria for the success of government legislation
   (lines 12–16)?
d Would Jeremy Bentham's principle of utility tend to increase or
   reduce government interference?
* e Who would make the decision as to whether government legislation
   would 'augment the happiness of the community' (line 15)?

4 Principles of Political Economy

'Laissez-faire', in short, should be the general practice: every departure
unless required by some great good, is a certain evil.

. . . We have observed that, as a general rule, the business of life is better
performed when those who have an immediate interest in it are left to
5   take their own course, unconditioned either by the mandate of the law or
by the meddling of any public functionary. The persons, or some of the
persons, who do the work, are likely to be better judges than the
government, of the means of attaining the particular end at which they
aim. Were we to suppose, what is not very probable, that the government
10   has possessed itself of the best knowledge which had been acquired up to a
given time by the persons most skilled in the occupation; even then, the
individual agents have so much stronger and more direct interest in the
result, that the means are far more likely to be improved and perfected if
left to their uncontrolled choice.

15   . . . Now any well-intentioned and tolerably civilized government may
think, without presumption, that it does or ought to possess a degree of
cultivation above the average of the community which it rules, and that it
should therefore be capable of offering better education and better
instruction to the people, than the greater number of them would
20   spontaneously demand. Education, therefore, is one of those things which

it is adviseable in principle that a government should provide for the people . . . .

J. S. Mill, *Principles of Political Economy*, Book V, ch. XI, 1909, pp 944−6

Questions

a What are the only circumstances under which 'laissez-faire' should be departed from in practice (lines 1−2)?

* b What problems could arise when deciding what would be the 'great good' (line 2)?

c Why, in practice, should the state not interfere (lines 3−9)?

d Why can government never be as effective as individual effort (lines 9−14)?

e What should the state interfere with on a large scale (lines 15−22)? Why should the government have this right?

* f If an exception is to be made in the case of education, in what other areas have government the legitimate right to interfere?

5 Corn Law and Poverty

Our opponents tell us that our object in bringing about the repeal of the Corn Laws, is, by reducing the price of corn, to lower the rate of their wages. I can only answer upon this point for the manufacturing districts; but, as far as they are concerned, I state it most emphatically as a truth,

5 that, for the last twenty years, whenever corn has been cheap wages have been high in Lancashire; and, on the other hand, when bread has been dear wages have been greatly reduced . . . .

Now, let me be fully understood as to what Free Traders really do want. We do not want cheap corn merely in order that we may have low

10 money prices. What we desire is plenty of corn, and we are utterly careless what its price is, provided we obtain it at the natural price. All we ask is, that corn shall follow the same law which the monopolists in food admit that labour must follow that 'it shall find its natural level in the markets of the world' . . . .

15 To pay for that corn, more manufactures would be required from this country; this would lead to an increased demand for labour in the manufacturing districts, which would necessarily be attended with a rise in wages, in order that the goods might be made for the purpose of exchanging for the corn brought from abroad . . . I observe there are

20 narrow-minded men in the agricultural districts, telling us, 'Oh, if you allow Free Trade, and bring in a quarter of corn from abroad, it is quite clear that you will sell one quarter less in England' . . . What! I would ask, if you set more people to work at better wages − if you can clear your streets of those spectres which are now haunting your thoroughfares

25 begging their daily bread − if you can depopulate your workhouses and

clear off the two million of paupers which now exist in the land, and put them to work at productive industry — do you not think that they would consume some of the wheat as well as you; and may not they be as we are now, consumers of wheaten bread by millions, instead of existing on their
30   present miserable dietary?

        R. Cobden, *Speeches*, 1870, 1, pp 118–133

Questions

a   What were the motives of the Anti-Corn Law League according to their opponents (lines 1–3)?

b   How does Cobden reply to this charge (lines 4–7)?

c   What does Cobden mean by the 'natural price' (line 11)?

d   According to Cobden, how are the 'monopolists in food' hypocritical (lines 11–14)?

e   How would the abolition of the Corn Laws expand the economy (lines 15–19)?

f   How would the abolition of the Corn Laws improve the welfare of the population (lines 23–30)?

*   g   What advances had the free traders made prior to the formation of the Anti-Corn Law League?

6   Repeal of the Corn Laws

15 May 1848

Sir, I do not rest my support of this bill upon the temporary ground of scarcity in Ireland . . . . Now all of you admit that the real question at issue is the improvement of the social and moral condition of the masses of the population; we wish to elevate in the gradation of society that great
5   class which gains its support by manual labour — that is agreed on all hands. The mere interests of the landlords — the mere interests of the occupying tenants, important as they are, are subordinate to the great question — which is calculated to improve the condition, and elevate the social character of the millions who subsist by manual labour, whether
10   they are engaged in manufactures or in agriculture? . . . I wish to convince them that our object has been so to apportion taxation, that we shall relieve industry and labour from any undue burden, and transfer it, so far as is consistent with the public good, to those who are better enabled to bear it.

        R. Peel, *Speeches*, IV, pp 689–96

Questions

a   What is the 'scarcity in Ireland' which Peel refutes as being the prime force for the repeal of the Corn Laws (line 2)?

b   According to Peel, what is everyone agreed upon as to the reasons for supporting the bill (lines 2–6)?

c How has Peel attempted to justify the repeal of the Corn Laws in respect of the unity of the country (lines 6 – 8)?

d What is the principle underlying the system of taxation that Peel advocates (lines 10 – 14)?

* *e* Why has Peel made no reference to the principles of free trade in his speech?

* *f* Why was the Anti-Corn Law League successful?

7 Limited Liability

Whatever success such unincorporated companies enjoyed, and however well legal disabilities were repaired in the opening decades of the nineteenth century, the liability of all partners remained unlimited. The inevitable consequence was that 'no prudent man (could) . . . invest his
5 surplus in any business that he (could not) himself practically superintend.'[1] The principle of limited liability was finally adopted in 1855 only after heated debate, but it is significant that the initial impetus to change was provided by 'a group of middle class philanthropists, most of whom accepted the title of Christian Socialists', who wished to create 'facilities
10 to safe investments for the savings of the middle and working class',[2] and by London financial interests which sought profitable industrial outlets for potential investors, not by those who argued in terms of freedom of contract nor by the industrialists themselves, whose voices were seldom heard in the discussions that preceded the Joint Stock Companies Acts of
15 1856 and 1862.

The response of the industrialists to this legislation confirms their muted interest. By 1885 limited companies account for, at most, between five and ten percent of the total number of important business organisations, and only in shipping, iron and steel, and cotton could their
20 influence be said to have been considerable. Although the firms that were limited were by far the most important in their spheres of activity, judged by size of unit and amount of fixed capital, the vast majority of the manufacturing firms of the country continued to be family businesses in the mid 1880s. Nevertheless, by the mid 1860s a legal structure existed in
25 Great Britain which made fundamental changes in the structure of the individual enterprise possible. The way was open for the emergence of the corporate economy, even though few trod the path.

P. L. Payne, *British Entrepreneurship in the Nineteenth Century*, 1974, pp 19 – 20

Questions

a Why were people reluctant to invest in enterprises in the first half of the nineteenth century (lines 3 – 6)?

1 B. C. Hunt, *The Development of the Business Corporation in Britain 1867 – 1880*, 1936
2 J. Saville, 'Sleeping Partnership and Limited Liability, 1850 – 56', *Economic History Review*, 1956, 2nd series, VIII

b Where did the stimulus come from for the adoption of the principle of limited liability (lines 7–11)?
c Which groups were noticeable by their absence (lines 12–13)?
d Which industries adopted limited liability status (lines 19–20)?
e What remained the usual form of business organisation late into the nineteenth century (lines 22–4)?
f What long term change in business organisation was possible after 1860 (lines 24–7)?
* g What commercial restrictions existed prior to the 1850s and why?

8 Made in Germany

Take observations, Gentle Reader, in your own surroundings . . . . You will find that the material of some of your own clothes was probably woven in Germany. Still more probable is it that some of your wife's garments are German importations; while it is practically beyond a doubt
5 that the magnificient mantles and jackets wherein her maids array themselves on Sundays out are German-made and German sold, for only so could they be done at the figure. Your governess's fiancé is a clerk in the City; but he was also made in Germany; nay, the material of your favourite (Patriotic) newspaper had the same birthplace as like as not.
10 Roam the house over, and the fateful mark will greet you at every turn, from the piano in your drawing-room to the mug on your kitchen dresser, blazoned though it be with the legend, 'A Present from Margate'. Descend to your domestic depths, and you shall find your very drain-pipes German made. You pick out of the grate the paper wrappings from
15 a book consignment, and they also are 'Made in Germany'. You stuff them into the fire, and reflect that the poker in your hand was forged in Germany . . . . And so the story goes on until, . . you drop off to sleep only to dream that St. Peter, (with a duly stamped halo round his head and a bunch of keys from the Rhineland), has refused you admission into
20 Paradise, because you bear not the mark of the Beast upon your forehead, and are not made in Germany.

E. E. Williams, *Made in Germany*, 1896, p 10

Questions

* a Why were Britain's economic fortunes changing in the last quarter of the nineteenth century? (see IX *Depression and Decline?* p 97)
b According to the extract, who is Britain's biggest competitor?
c How completely have German-made articles replaced British?
d What examples of emotive language does Williams use?
e What does Williams mean, 'he was also made in Germany' (line 8)?
f Why should Germany have become such a powerful competitor?

9 Reactions to Chamberlain's Speech (1903)

In the few hours (after Chamberlain's speech of 15th May) England, and indeed the whole Empire, were in a ferment of indescribable excitement. In teaching his countrymen to think imperially Chamberlain had builded better than he knew. . . . In its protest against the intolerable tyranny of a
5 meaningless economic formula, the speech kindled into instant flame all the embers of doubt and suspicion about the infallibility of Free Trade, which had been silently smouldering for years.

Men who on 15th May would have resented being described as anything but Free Traders, found themselves within a few days hating
10 Free Trade with all the intensity with which any Calvinist ever hated the Church of Rome. On the other hand, many who would have accepted a preferential reduction of the corn duties with indifference, or even satisfaction, suddenly shrank back in dismay from the terrifying vista now opening out to their sight. A complete remoulding, not only of
15 British policy, but, harder still, of their intellectual outlook, and of their whole mental stock-in-trade of familiar and comforting phrases and formulas – instinct bade them avert at all costs such a disaster. Add to this intellectual ferment the fierce hunger of an Opposition long cheated of its hopes of office, and looking eagerly for some topic to close its own ranks
20 and break up those of its opponents, the anxious shepherding of Government party managers only intent on preventing a dissolution, and the individual ambitions of rising politicians, and it becomes possible to form some conception of the confused struggle which now began – a struggle which coloured even when it did not dominate, English politics
25 for decades, and in the course of which the original object of Chamberlain's policy seemed at times to be almost forgotten by those who professed to be his followers. . . .

L. S. Amery, *My Political Life*, i, pp 236–40

Questions

a What 'meaningless economic formula' had Chamberlain referred to in his speech (line 5)?

b What phrase indicates the intensity of feeling over the issue of free trade?

c Why did so many find the idea of imperial preference difficult to accept (lines 14–17)?

d How did Chamberlain's speech assist the Opposition (lines 17–22)?

e What were the long term political repercussions of Chamberlain's speech (lines 23–7)?

* *f* Why did the Protectionist movement ally with Imperialism?

10 The Ideology of Laissez-Faire

A widespread development of free trade ideology developed in mid-nineteenth-century England, but a similar laissez-faire ideology did not. A large part of the error which the historiography contains in its categorization of the period as one of laissez-faire is due to a false
5 identification of laissez-faire and free trade. It is striking how often one finds the two phrases used synonymously by later writers. Even today, one sometimes finds the same identification in the writing of historians who have steeped themselves deeply in the literature of the mid-Victorian age. More than anything else, it is responsible for the fact that
10 the myth continues to draw fitful breath despite the blows that scholarship has rained upon it in recent years.

Free trade = laissez-faire is a false equation, but this is not to deny that free trade was a policy of non-intervention. Moreover, it was a policy of non-intervention in an area of national concern that was far from minor.
15 The point is that, however important it was, international trade was nevertheless a particular area of economic activity and therefore free trade was a particular policy; whereas laissez-faire is a general theory of economic policy applicable, as 'The Economist' exemplified, to all particular cases.

H. Scott Gordon, 'The Ideology of Laissez-Faire' in A. W. Coats, (ed.) *The Classical Economists and Economic Policy*, pp 202 – 3

Questions

a According to H. Scott Gordon what basic mistake in definition have historians made (lines 3 – 6)?

b What is the distinction between free trade and laissez-faire (lines 12 – 18)?

c What do the two terms have in common (lines 12 – 14)?

* d Can the term laissez-faire be appropriately applied in the field of economic activity during the period 1815 – 1870?

Further reading

A. W. Coats, (ed.) *The Classical Economists and Economic Policy (1971)*; P. L. Payne, *British Entrepreneurship in the Nineteenth Century* (1974); O. MacDonagh, *Early Victorian Government 1830 – 1870* (1977); A. J. Taylor, *Laissez-Faire and State Intervention in Nineteenth-century Britain* (1972).

V Laissez-Faire and State Intervention: Social Management

Introduction

The King's ministers in early nineteenth-century Britain were in no doubt about their brief to govern: rule rather than legislate. They had to manage the affairs of monarchy, see to the defence of the realm, conduct foreign affairs, create revenue and enable local officials to maintain the peace, providing the necessary stability for society to function as it always had done. This was the mantle handed down by the Augustan Age, one which had grown heavier through preceding eras. It was a mantle which fitted well with the political suit of clothes fashioned in the style of laissez-faire philosophy.

State intervention by social legislation has led some historians to question the usefulness of the phrase laissez-faire to describe an age in which the State's role is so obvious. In reaching an answer to such a question, it is important not to lose sight of the character of the legislation enacted.

To intervene in order to maintain social stability was quite in keeping with traditional governmental responsibility. The Poor Law Commission is a case in point, a response to the complaints of those whose responsibility to deal with poverty was centuries old, a response which cost the Exchequer little, a response which has been monumentally criticised for what it did *not* do. The advocates of Factory Reform and Sanitary Legislation made social well-being, order, morality and the rectitude of property and station main planks in their platforms. Government could act in its traditional role by legislating in such areas and did so, but with reluctance and an eye on order and economy, even after 1867 when winning the votes of labouring men.

Furthermore, it is important to remember that 1800-1900 was an age of the entrepreneur and great individuals. Many of these held strong views on the philosophy of laissez-faire and were conscious of governmental action. Despite the fact that other codes, philosophies and influences were also at work, the nature of the legislation and explicit motivation of contemporaries do not allow laissez-faire to be easily dismissed.

1 Problems of the Industrial City

The worst aspects of nineteenth-century urban growth are reasonably well known. The great industrial cities came into existence on the new economic foundations laid in the eighteenth century with the growth in population and the expansion of industry. The pressure of rapidly
5 increasing numbers of people and the social consequences of the introduction of new industrial techniques and new ways of organizing work involved a sharp break with the past. The fact that the new techniques were introduced by private enterprise and that the work was organized for other people not by them largely determined the reaction
10 to the break.

The industrial city was bound to be a place of problems. Economic individualism and common civic purpose were difficult to reconcile. The priority of industrial discipline in shaping all human relations was bound to make other aspects of life seem secondary. A high rate of industrial
15 investment might mean not only a low rate of consumption and a paucity of social investment but a total indifference to social costs . . . .

. . . Lack of general concern for social costs was related to the pressures not only of urbanization but of industrialization. The city offered external economies to the businessman: it was all too easy to forget that
20 the economies entailed social costs as well. In a new industrial society belief in private property survived as the foundation of the whole social system. The belief was sustained by the law. It had also shaped eighteenth and early nineteenth-century schemes of improvement. When Victorian legislation was passed which tampered with the rights of private
25 property, it was always contentious and difficult to implement . . . .

. . . Throughout the Victorian age the most effective argument for sanitary reform was that it would actually save money in the long run, not squander it. 'Civic economy' was a branch of political economy . . . .

. . . Social conditions in the new communities encouraged both the
30 amassing of facts and the airing of viewpoints. However great the resistance, there was persistent pressure to control social change . . . .

Asa Briggs, *Victorian Cities*, 1968, pp 18, 21, 23−4

Questions

a According to the writer, what was the origin of cities (lines 2−4)?

b What important factor does Briggs identify as being crucial to the response to urban growth (lines 7−10)?

c Why were cities likely to present problems (lines 11−16)?

d What factor shaped the attitude of legislators in the nineteenth century (lines 17−25)?

*
e Which problems facing nineteenth-century governments were presented by the urbanisation of society?

2 Contemporary Opposition to Government Legislation

If there be in Mr Southey's[1] political system any leading principle, any one error which diverges more widely and variously than any other, it is that of which his theory about national works is a ramification. He conceives that the business of the magistrate is not merely to see that the
5 persons and property of the people are secure from attack, but that he ought to be a jack-of-all-trades, — architect, engineer, schoolmaster, merchant, theologian, a Lady Bountiful in every parish, a Paul Pry in every house, spying, eavesdropping, relieving, admonishing, spending our money for us, and choosing our opinions for us. His principle is, if we
10 understand it rightly, that no man can do anything so well for himself as his rulers, be they who they may, can do it for him, and that a government approaches nearer and nearer to perfection, in proportion as it interferes more and more with the habits and notions of individuals.

Macaulay, *Critical Essays*, 1829

Questions

a What does Macaulay mean by the term 'national works' (line 3)?
b What function does Macaulay think ought to be provided by a magistrate (lines 4—5)?
c Express in your own words what Macaulay feared (lines 7—9).
d On what main ground does Macaulay attack collectivism (lines 9—11)?
* *e* Who were the main proponents of 'laissez-faire' 1800—1870?

3 The Poor Law Report 1834

It may be assumed that in the administration of relief, the public is warranted in imposing such conditions on the individual relieved, as are conducive to the benefit either of the individual himself, or of the country at large, at whose expense he is to be relieved.
5 The first and most essential of all conditions, a principle which we find universally admitted, even by those whose practice is at variance with it, is that his situation on the whole shall not be made really or apparently so eligible as the situation of the independent labourer of the lowest class. Throughout the evidence it is shown, that in proportion as the condition
10 of any pauper is elevated above the condition of independent labourers, the condition of the independent class is depressed; their industry is impaired, their employment becomes unsteady, and its remuneration in wages is diminished. Such persons, therefore, are under the strongest inducements to quit the less eligible class of labourers and enter the more

---

1 Author of 'Colloquies on the Progress and Prospects of Society' and an advocate of collectivism

15 eligible class of paupers. The converse is the effect when the pauper class is placed in its proper position, below the condition of the independent labourer. Every penny bestowed, that tends to render the condition of the paupers more eligible than that of the independent labourer, is a bounty on indolence and vice. We have found, that as the poor's rates are at
20 present administered, they operate as bounties of this description to the amount of several millions annually. . . .

     . . . We recommend, therefore, the appointment of a Central Board to control the administration of the Poor Laws; with such assistant Commissioners as may be found requisite; and that the Commissioners be
25 empowered and directed to frame and enforce regulations for the government or workhouses, and as to the nature and amount of relief to be given and the labour to be exacted in them, and that such regulations shall, as far as may be practicable, be uniform throughout the country. . . .
30   . . . To effect these purposes we recommend that the Central Board be empowered to cause any number of parishes which they may think convenient to be incorporated for the purpose of workhouse management, and for providing new workhouses where necessary . . . .

        The Poor Law Report, 1834, pp 228, 297, 314

Questions

a Why did the Commissioners assume that those responsible for discharging poor relief could impose conditions on the recipients (lines 1 – 4)?
b What did the Commissioners take as their first principle and on what grounds (lines 5 – 17)?
c What was their main fear if such a principle was not followed (lines 17 – 21)?
d What recommendations did the Commissioners make (lines 22 – 33)?
* e Explain why the Poor Law Commission was undertaken.
* f What were the shortcomings of the 1834 Poor Law Report?

4   The Inadequacy of the Poor Law

Whatever their importance in administrative history, the Report of the Royal Commission on the Poor Laws, and the Act which followed hard on its heels, contained weaknesses which severely limited their usefulness in dealing with poverty, or even with pauperism, in the second half of the
5 nineteenth century. In the first place, the Royal Commission had concentrated too much of its attention upon a single problem, that of the able-bodied unemployed, particularly in rural areas, who it feared were being demoralised by ill-conceived grants of outdoor relief. It paid too little regard to the problems of those who were pauperised because of
10 physical or mental ill-health, old age or loss of parents, although these

probably constituted by far the largest proportion of those on relief. The important and complex problem of settlement received only cursory treatment in the Report and was only modified in a few minor details by the Act, and the vital question of rating and the finance of poor relief was
15 dealt with in an equally cavalier fashion. These were questions which were to harass poor law administrators and social reformers for the next hundred years. Secondly, the reformers of 1834 focused their attention upon the problem of rural poverty, and produced the machinery to deal with it. Yet the problem of the future was to be the far more difficult one
20 of urban, industrial poverty.
The poor law proved to be ill-adapted for dealing with poverty, and thus was increasingly ignored as a device for social reform . . . the oversimplified early nineteenth-century view of poverty was broken down by investigation of the causes of poverty, and by changing attitudes
25 towards it, a process which led to the introduction of new methods of treating poverty.

M. E. Rose, *The Relief of Poverty 1834–1914*, 1972, p 12

Questions

a According to the writer, what was the intrinsic fault of the 1834 Poor Law (lines 1–5)?
b What major mistake did the Commissioners make (lines 6–8)?
c Which sections of the poor were really overlooked (lines 8–11)?
d What major problem did the Commissioners fail to see (lines 17–20)?
* *e* Why was the 1834 Poor Law so inadequate?
* *f* What were the consequences and effects of the 1834 Poor Law?

5 Further Criticisms of the Poor Law

The Old Poor Law, with its use of outdoor relief to assist the underpaid was, in essence, a device for dealing with the problem of surplus labour in the lagging rural sector of a rapidly expanding but still underdeveloped economy. And considering the quality of social administration in the day,
5 it was by no means an unenlightened policy. The Poor Law Commissioners of 1834 thought otherwise and deliberately selected the facts so as to impeach the existing administration on pre-determined lines. Not only did they fail in any way to take account of the special problem of structural unemployment in the countryside, but what evidence they
10 did present consisted of little more than picturesque anecdotes of maladministration. Even the elaborate questionnaire which they circulated among the parishes was never analysed or reduced to summary form. No attempt was made to make a census of the poor, and to this day we know more about the nature and composition of the pauper host in
15 1802 than in 1834. Anyone who has read the *Report of 1834* can testify to the overwhelming cumulative effect of the endless recital of ills from the

mouths of squires, magistrates, overseers, and clergymen. But as evidence of a social malady it has little value, particularly on the ultimate question of the corrupting influence of lavish relief; . . .

20 . . . No wonder the 'harsh but salutary Act' fell short, at nearly every point, of effecting sweeping reform. Gradually . . . the 'principles of 1834' were undermined in practice by the administration of successive governments, while competing public services increasingly took over the functions of the Poor Law.

M. Blaug, 'The Myth of the Old Poor Law', *Essays in Social History*, (eds) M. W. Flinn and T. C. Smout, 1974, pp 143−4

Questions

a What function does the writer see the Old Poor Law as having provided (lines 1−4)?

b Of what major crime does the writer accuse the Poor Law Commissioners (lines 6−7)?

c What were the failures of the Poor Law Commissioners (lines 8−13)?

d Why does the writer think that the 1834 Report has little value as an *accurate* social document (lines 15−19)?

* e What provisions were made for the relief of poverty before 1834?

* f How was the 1834 Poor Law undermined during the nineteenth century?

6 The Factory Act 1833

(a) I That . . . no Person under Eighteen Years of Age shall be allowed to work in the Night, (that is to say,) between the Hours of Half past Eight o'Clock in the Evening and Half past Five o'Clock in the Morning, except as herein-after provided, in or about any Cotton, Woollen,
5 Worsted, Hemp, Flax, Tow, Linen, or Silk Mill or Factory wherein Steam or Water or any other mechanical Power is or shall be used to propel or work the Machinery in such Mill or Factory . . . situated in any Part of the United Kingdom . . . .

II That no Person under the Age of Eighteen Years shall be employed in
10 any such Mill or Factory . . . more than Twelve Hours in Any One Day, nor more than Sixty-Nine hours in Any One Week . . . .

VIII . . . It shall not be lawful for any Person whatsoever to employ, keep, or allow to remain in any Factory or Mill . . . for a longer Time than Forty-eight Hours in any One Week, nor for a longer Time than
15 Nine Hours in any One Day . . . any Child who shall not have completed his or her Eleventh Year of Age . . . .

XVII . . . It shall be lawful for His Majesty . . . to appoint . . . Four Persons to be Inspectors of Factories and Places where the Labour of

Children and young Persons under Eighteen Years of Age is
20 employed . . . .
        Lord Althorp's Factory Act, 29 August, 1833

(b) . . . I see a decided change for the better within the last three months;
for the strong dislike to the Act, which existed among a large number of
the most respectable mill-owners, has greatly subsided. From what I have
seen, and from the opinions I have heard expressed by them and their
25 work-people, there is evidently an increased conviction on the minds of
both that an effective interference of the Legislature, for the protection of
the children employed in factories is necessary, and that it is a just
principle; . . .
        From a report by Leonard Horner, Factory Inspector,
        Parliamentary Papers, 1837

Questions

a   What limitations did the 1833 Act place on the employment of
    children (lines 1 – 16)?
b   Why is clause XVII so important? How effective do you think this
    provision was for the enforcement of the Act?
c   What had been the reaction to the Act by 1837 (lines 21 – 8)?
d   Why did the framers of the Act limit the total number of hours
    worked in one week?
e   Why did early factory legislation apply only to textile mills?
* f   Assess the factors which were important in the achievement of factory
    legislation in the nineteenth century.

7   The Ten Hour Bill 1846

. . . Among all the alterations that have been effected since the year 1833,
I am sorry to perceive that nothing has been done for the benefit of young
persons between the ages of thirteen and eighteen . . . now a very large
portion of them are females, and I think I may appeal to the House to say,
5   whether it is not cruel to take a young female on the very day on which
she has passed the age of thirteen, at the most tender period of her life, and
to demand of her precisely the same work in duration . . . which is
demanded from ripe and vigorous manhood? . . . how is it possible that
they should learn the details of domestic life which constitute the comfort
10 of the working man's home, and contribute so powerfully to the
morality of the rising generation . . . ? . . . Sir, we must not shut out of
our view the wide surface of society to be affected by our decision . . . it
will be a fatal night whenever you decide adversely, for you will have
closed all hopes of moral, and even of secular improvement to multitudes
15 of the young and helpless. And will this not tend to widen the
interval . . . that separates the rich from the poorer sort? . . . The

overtoiled operatives, both as children and adults, are alone excluded
from the common advantage; a few, it is true, of special genius, may
triumph over every opposing obstacle; but the mass are abandoned to a
20 state of things in which moral and intellectual culture, forethought and
economy, and the resources of independent action, are far beyond their
means. . . . This, surely, is an unsound and fearful position; the contrast is
seen, felt, and resented; . . . property and station become odious, because
they are founded on acquirements from which the multitudes are
25 excluded by the prevailing system.
Lord Ashley, Introduction of the Ten Hour Bill, 1846,
Parliamentary Debates, 29 January, 1846

Questions

a What limitation of the 1833 factory legislation did Ashley highlight
(lines 1 – 3)?
b Why did he think it important that young adolescent girls should be
catered for in factory legislation (lines 8 – 11)?
c What did he think would be the consequences of ignoring the
problem of young girls in factories (lines 13 – 16)?
d Why did he feel it imperative to expand the existing factory
legislation (lines 17 – 25)?
* e What were the pressures bearing on government to cause social
legislation by 1848?

8 Report on the Sanitary Conditions of the Labouring Population 1842

. . . That the various forms of epidemic, endemic, and other disease
caused, or aggravated, or propagated chiefly amongst the labouring
classes by atmospheric impurities produced by decomposing animal and
vegetable substances, by damp and filth, and close and overcrowded
5 dwellings prevail amongst the population in every part of the kingdom,
whether dwelling in separate houses, in rural villages, in small towns, in
the larger towns – as they have been found to prevail in the lowest
districts of the metropolis.
. . . That the population so exposed . . . is less susceptible of moral
10 influences, and the effects of education are more transient than with a
healthy population.
That these above circumstances tend to produce an adult population
short-lived, improvident, reckless, and intemperate, and with habitual
avidity for sensual gratifications.
15 That these habits lead to the abandonment of all conveniences and
decencies of life, and especially lead to the overcrowding of their homes,
which is destructive to the morality as well as the health of large classes of
both sexes.

That defective town cleansing fosters habits of the most abject
20 degradation and tends to the demoralisation of large numbers of human
beings, who subsist by means of what they find amidst the noxious filth
accumulated in neglected streets and by-places.

That the expenses of local public works are in general unequally and
unfairly assessed, oppressively and uneconomically collected, by separate
25 collections, wastefully expended in separate and inefficient operations by
unskilled and practically irresponsible officers.

That the existing law for the protection of the public health and the
constitutional machinery for reclaiming its execution, such as the Courts
Leet, have fallen into desuetude, and are in the state indicated by the
30 prevalence of the evils they were intended to prevent.

Edwin Chadwick, *Report on the Sanitary Condition of the Labouring
Population*, 1842, Conclusions

Questions

a According to Chadwick, in what conditions did the working classes
   live (lines 1–8)?
b What were the effects of those conditions on the people who endured
   them (lines 9–22)?
c What was the main failing in dealing with the problems (lines 23–6)?
d Why was existing law useless (lines 27–30)?
* *e* Why was the Public Health Act of 1848 passed?
* *f* What were the results of the 1848 legislation up to 1870?

9 Samuel Smiles – a surprising advocate of government legislation

When typhus or cholera breaks out, they tell us that nobody is to blame.
That terrible Nobody! How much he has to answer for! More mischief is
done by Nobody than by all the world besides. Nobody adulterates our
food. Nobody poisons us with bad drink. Nobody supplies us with foul
5 water. Nobody spreads fever in blind alleys and unswept lanes. Nobody
leaves towns undrained. Nobody fills jails, penitentiaries and convict
stations. Nobody makes poachers, thieves and drunkards.

Nobody has a theory, too – a dreadful theory. It is embodied in two
words: Laissez-faire – Let alone. When people are poisoned by plaster of
10 Paris mixed with flour, 'Let alone' is the remedy. When *Cocculus Indicus*
is used instead of hops, and men die prematurely, it is easy to say,
'Nobody did it'. Let those who can, find out when they are cheated:
Caveat emptor. When people live in foul dwellings, let them alone. Let
wretchedness do its work; do not interfere with death.

Samuel Smiles, *Thrift*, 1889, pp 358–9

Questions

a   What social evils has Smiles outlined (lines 1−7)?

b   What did Smiles blame for the prevalence of so many ills (lines 8−9)?

*   *c*   What fundamental social principle is attacked in lines 11−14?

  d   What improvements to urban living conditions were achieved between 1800 and 1900?

*   *e*   Why do you find this argument unusual coming from Samuel Smiles?

10   Report on the 1875 Public Health Act

No less than 29 sanitary measures have been enacted since the Health of Towns Commission of 1846. In this uncodified state, these Acts naturally displayed much confusion, redundancy and apparent confusion. They had been made at different times, by various hands, and with various
5   objects. Some were permissive, some compulsory, some partly the one and partly the other. Each dealt with some special part of the subject, but none could be said to define its departments clearly and exhaustively . . . Part 3, representing the main bulk of the Act, and occupying 131 clauses, consists of what are specially denominated
10   sanitary provisions. It is divided into the heads of: 1, sewerage and drainage; 2, privies, water-closets etc.; 3, scavenging and cleansing; 4, water supply; 5, regulation of cellar dwellings and lodging houses; 6, nuisances; 7, offensive trades; 8, unsound meat etc.; 9, infectious diseases and hospitals; 10, prevention of epidemic diseases; 11, mortuaries. The
15   objects thus miscellaneously grouped are apparently arranged for the convenience and information of those whose duty it is to carry the Act into effect. Each head includes the corresponding statutory regulations, together with the penalties by which they are severally to be enforced. Part 4 is specially entitled 'Local Government Provisions' and contains,
20   under several heads, the law upon such matters of local government as are only indirectly connected with the question of public health. Under this title we have − 1, Regulations with regard to highways and streets, including the power for widening, improving, paving and lighting them; 2, public pleasure grounds, under which head stands, somewhat oddly,
25   the power to provide urban districts with public clocks; 3, markets and slaughter houses; 4, police regulations. . . .

        The Times, 25 August, 1875

Questions

a   What was the main reason for the 1875 Health Act (lines 1−8)?

b   What did the main part of the Act contain (lines 10−14)?

c   How was the legislation arranged (lines 15−18)?

d What provisions were made for local government to improve the health of the environment (lines 22−6)?

* *e* What was the importance of the 1875 Health Act?

11 What was 'laissez-faire'? Toward an explanation

It is therefore in the field of social and still more of economic policy that the idea of an age of *laissez-faire* can be most fairly tested . . . the more purely economic the area of governmental concern, the more strongly evident is the adoption of policies which can be legitimately described as
5   *laissez-faire*. Conversely, where economic considerations are, or appear to be, subordinate, less weight is seen to be placed on *laissez-faire* prescription . . . .

Even in those areas of social policy, however, where state intervention was least inhibited by considerations of economic individualism, the
10 limitations of governmental action are readily discernible. Intervention was prompted not by any conviction of its innate desirability but by the inescapable need to meet pressing problems, created largely by the twin forces of industrialisation and urbanisation, which were incapable of individualist solutions. The governments of early and mid-Victorian
15 England did not so much seek to provide new remedies for old problems as to come to terms with the new crises which accompanied a rapidly changing social order. Although Parliament legislated widely and purposefully and the bureaucracy worked powerfully and at times heroically within the limits which successive governments set for it,
20 Victorian social policy was basically negative and unconstructive. If the origins of the Welfare State are to be traced to the nineteenth century, the gestation period was long; in little over a decade the Edwardians accomplished more than the Victorians had achieved in two-thirds of a century.
25 Such welfare services as the Victorian state provided were furnished at small cost to the central Exchequer . . . .

Victorian governments, like the Classical economists, had no explicit theory of economic growth. But implicitly they believed that an economy thrives best when left to the free play of market forces. In this
30 respect, therefore, the commitment to *laissez-faire* was positive . . . .

A. J. Taylor, *Laissez-faire and State Intervention in Nineteenth-century Britain*, 1972, pp 55, 56, 60

Questions

a In which area of governmental concern does the writer feel 'laissez-faire' to be most readily discernible (lines 1−7)?

b Why does the writer think that 'laissez-faire' was also at work in social legislation (lines 8−14)?

c How is Victorian legislation placed in perspective (lines 21−6)?

    d What are 'market forces' (line 29)?

*   *e* Can the period 1800–1900 be described as an age of 'laissez-faire'?

*   *f* How useful is 'laissez-faire' as a concept in which to frame nineteenth-century social legislation?

Further reading

Asa Briggs, *Victorian Cities* (1968); E. C. Midwinter, *Victorian Social Reform* (1968); D. Roberts, *Victorian Origins of the Welfare State* (1960); J. B. Brebner, 'Laissez-faire and state intervention in nineteenth-century Britain', *Journal of Economic History*, 8, (1948); A. J. Taylor, *Laissez-faire and State Intervention in Nineteenth-century Britain* (1972).

VI Education

Introduction

An 1870 Punch cartoon depicts W. E. Forster addressing five urchins: 'Well, my little people, we have been gravely and earnestly considering whether you may learn to read. I am happy to tell you that, subject to a variety of restrictions, conscience clauses, and the consent of your vestries – you may!' In retrospect, Forster's Act can be seen as the fulcrum of nineteenth-century educational development; despite the cartoonist's barb, it provided viable answers to the two main questions which had bedevilled the issue from the beginning of the century:

1   To what extent ought the poor to be educated, assuming that they should be?
2   What form of provision was needed to effect it, a national or a voluntary system?

The Act thereby opened the future to further rationalisation of the role of the State vis-à-vis educational structure.

In the early years of the century the call to educate the poor came, for different reasons, from Radicals and churchmen. It was a concept central to the philosophies of Bentham and Mill. The churchmen had put their ideas into operation by 1815, albeit in rival societies. By the time that real State intervention in the education field was being advocated, the rapid growth of the Church schemes and subsequent sectarian variations had become a seemingly intractable doctrinal obstacle to any government initiative in establishing a national system of schools.

Despite the early manifestation of the education debate, it was only gradually that government became involved. Whitbread's 1807 Bill and the Select Committees of 1816–1818 revealed an interest, but only in 1833 was the first government grant made, a delay which demonstrated government's reluctance to assume direct responsibility. The grant, nevertheless, served to enmesh the government as annual expenditure grew and an inspectorate was needed to check for misuse of funds. The attitude remained that even if government was to be involved, a minimum of taxpayers' money ought to be used. The Revised Code of 1862 made sure that if education was inefficient, it would be also cheap, for government grants were to be paid according to results, following the recommendation of the Newcastle Commission – called into being once the government had established a permanent Education Department as a Committee in Council. Legislative initiative in the establishment of schools was still avoided.

Direct legislation was made inevitable by a combination of growing foreign, technical and industrial competition and the extension of the franchise. Even then, Forster demonstrated government's reluctance to assume full responsibility by producing an Act 'to fill up gaps'.

The balance was tipped. As the short and long term inadequacies of the 1870 Act were revealed, with an increasingly literate and potentially volatile electorate, remedial legislation established the basis of a uniform system of education, overseen from a government department and based on an educational philosophy which owed as much to ideas about social control as the universal fulfilment of academic potential.

1 Forster's Speech Introducing The Education Bill 1870

. . . though we have done well in assisting the benevolent gentlemen who have established schools, yet the result of the State leaving the initiative to volunteers is, that where State help has been most wanted, State help has been least given, and that where it was desirable that State
5 power should be most felt it was not felt at all . . . . Therefore, notwithstanding the large sums of money we have voted, we find a vast number of children badly taught, or utterly untaught, because there are too few schools and too many bad schools . . . . Hence comes a demand from all parts of the country for a complete system of national
10 education . . . .

Our object is to complete the present voluntary system, to fill up gaps, sparing the public money where it can be done without . . . .

Now I will at once proceed to the main principles . . . . They are two in number. Legal enactment, that there will be efficient schools
15 everywhere throughout the kingdom. Compulsory provision of such schools if and where needed, but not unless proved to be needed . . . .

Upon the speedy provision of elementary education depends our industrial prosperity . . . .

Now that we have given them* political power we must not wait any
20 longer to give them education.

Speech by Mr. W. E. Forster introducing the Elementary Education Bill in the House of Commons, 17th February 1870

Questions

a What is Forster's main criticism of the system of elementary education before 1870 (lines 2–5)?

b How did Forster intend to remedy the defects he criticised?

* the people

* c What were Forster's grounds for urgent state intervention beyond the
remedying of existing defects?
*   d What were arguments for and against a national system of education
raised prior to 1870?
*   e What were the strengths and weaknesses of the 1870 Education Act?

2 The Need to Teach the Poor 1821

From their dependent situation, the poor are peculiarly the objects of the
care and attention of the higher classes of the community: if they are
suffered to grow up in ignorance and vice, a fearful responsibility will lie
upon those who might have prevented it: that vice follows in the train of
5 ignorance will not now be disputed. The cultivation of the mind
bestowed in these elementary schools, . . . inspires them with sentiments
favourable to virtue, and habituates them to subordination and
control . . . instances are not wanting in which parents have become
reformed characters, in consequence of their children being admitted to
10 the schools.
    The middle and upper ranks of society are now more dependent upon
the poor than without a little reflection they are yet aware of: it is to the
labour and skill of the poor that we owe our comforts and conveniences:
we indeed have a deep interest in the state of their morals, . . . and, what
15 is of still greater importance, the minds of our children may be materially
influenced by the good or bad qualities of the servants in whose care they
frequently spend so much of their time. The higher ranks of society are
then deeply interested in providing a moral and religious education for
the whole of the poor.
    Manual of Teaching, 1821

Questions

a What is the evidence for a developing inter-dependence of social
classes?
b What practical reasons are given for educating the poor?
c What emphasis does the writer of the document stress in the type of
education to be provided for the poor?
*   d In what ways does nineteenth-century education appear to con-
centrate on the political control of the labouring classes?

3 Whitbread's Education Bill 1807

Davies Giddy . . . giving education to the labouring classes of the poor,
would, in effect, be found to be prejudicial to their morals and happiness;
it would lead them to despise their lot in life, instead of making them
good servants in agriculture and other laborious employments to which
5 their rank in society had destined them; instead of teaching them
subordination it would render them factious and refractory, as was

evident in the manufacturing counties; it would enable them to read seditious pamphlets, vicious books, and publications against Christianity; it would render them insolent to their superiors; . . . Besides, if the Bill
10   were to pass into law, it would go to burden the country with a most enormous and incalculable expense, and to load the industrious orders of society with still heavier imposts . . . .

Mr Rose . . . had no doubt that the poor ought to be taught to read; as to writing, he had some doubt, because those who had learnt to write well
15   were not willing to abide at the plough, but looked to a situation in some counting house.

Debate on Whitbread's Bill, 1807

Questions

a   How does Giddy show that educating the poor is not in the interests of the upper social strata?

b   What practical reasons does Giddy offer to reinforce his arguments against providing education for the poor?

c   Why does Mr Rose express particular objection to the teaching of writing (lines 15–16)?

*   d   What is significant about the timing of this debate?

*   e   What education provision had been made for the poor before 1800?

4   Opposition to Government Support in Education 1833

In the first place, sir, I have never either spoken or written against the lower classes being educated; . . . I have spoken against, written against, and shall speak and write against, laying a tax upon the people, though to the amount of one single farthing a head in twenty years, for the purpose of
5   promoting what is called 'education'. Never shall a vote to the amount of one penny pass for this purpose, without my dividing the House (of Commons) upon it. What! I lend my hand in taxing the industrious shoemaker, in order to make him pay for the education of the shoemaker who is not industrious? I *tax* the ploughman, make him pay a tax on his
10   beer, on his sugar, on his tobacco, to compel him to assist in what is called the educating of the children of the shirking slip-shod that has just been jostled into matrimony from behind the master's chair; I will do no such thing, even if I had no other objection than this, which is so consonant with justice and with common sense; but I have other and most powerful
15   objections, to *any plan* of 'national education', which must of necessity create a new and most terrific control in the hands of the Government. I am further of the opinion and I know it to be true, indeed, that such a thing must be most injurious, not only to the morals but to the liberties of the country; and I am ready to maintain these opinions against all the
20   doctrinaires and canters in the world.

William Cobbett, *The Political Register*, 21st September, 1833

Questions

a Why has Cobbett particular objections to education being funded out of taxation?

b Why is Cobbett opposed to the government being the exclusive provider of education?

* c Offer an explanation for the timing of the article.

* d From which quarters did extra-parliamentary pressure for increased state action in education emanate between 1815 and 1902?

5 Opposition to Government Support in Education 1834

Do you think that a system of primary education, established by law, would be beneficial?

I think that it is wholly inapplicable to the present condition of the country, and the actual state of education. Those who recommend it on
5 account of its successful adoption on the Continent, do not reflect upon the funds which it would require, and upon the exertions already made in this country by individual beneficence . . . Now, to establish and maintain such a number of schools, would be a most heavy expense . . . would cost £2 000 000 a year . . . .

10 *Do you consider that a compulsory education would be justified, either on principles of public utility or expediency?*

I am decidedly of opinion that it is justifiable upon neither; but, above all, I should regard anything of the kind as utterly destructive of the end it has in view. Suppose the people of England were taught to bear it, and to be
15 forced to educate their children by penalties, education would be made absolutely hateful in their eyes, and would speedily cease to be endured. They who have argued in favour of such a scheme from the example of a military government like that of Prussia, have betrayed, in my opinion, great ignorance of the nature of Englishmen . . . .

Evidence of the Lord Chancellor, Lord Brougham and Vaux to the Parliamentary Committee on the State of Education, 1834

Questions

a On what grounds is Lord Brougham sceptical of further state intervention?

b In what ways does Lord Brougham argue that compulsory schooling is alien to English tradition?

c According to Brougham what would be the results of compulsion?

* d In what ways did Brougham's concept of government responsibility reflect the traditional outlook of the role of government?

6 Education and Crime

It is, indeed, strange that with the facts of daily life before them in the street, in the counting-house, and in the family, thinking men should still expect education to cure crimes. If armies of teachers, regarded with a certain superstitious reverence, have been unable to purify society in all
5 these eighteen centuries, it is hardly likely that other armies of teachers, not so regarded, will be able to do it . . . . The expectation that crime may presently be cured, whether by State education, or the silent system, or the separate system, or any other system, is one of those Utopianisms fallen into by people who pride themselves on being practical.

H. Spencer, *Social Statics*

Questions

a What does Spencer imply about the status of teachers in the nineteenth century (lines 3−6)?

b Who does Spencer have in mind when he refers to 'one of the Utopianisms fallen into by people who pride themselves on being practical (lines 8−9)?

c What indication does Spencer give that education was a widespread concern?

* d What arguments did the Utilitarians raise in favour of educating the poor?

7 Notice advertising the Foundation of the British School for Girls 1840

In this School your Children (above Six Years of Age) will receive a sound Scriptural Education. The Principles on which this School is founded enable it to admit the Children of Parents of every Religious Denomination, while it teaches the Doctrines of Religion from the Page
5 of Divine Inspiration itself, (the introduction of the Sacred Scriptures, without Note or Comment, as the only Book of Religious Instruction, has been from the first a Fundamental Rule in all the Schools of the Society,) it excludes Creeds and Catechisms; and thus, occupying the ground of our Common Christianity, it acts as a Powerful Auxiliary to
10 Sabbath School Instruction, and leaves untouched the Formularies and Discipline of particular Churches.

The great object of the Promoters of these Schools being, that the Children may be Trained to Habits of Industry and Frugality in early life, the Girls will be allowed to bring with them their own Work to Make or
15 Repair.

It is required, that the Girls come to School with their Hands and Faces Clean, their Hair Combed, and their Clothes Whole.

Instructions will be given in Reading, Writing, Arithmetic, Grammar,

and Needlework. Mothers will be allowed to send their elder Girls for
20 half a day if more convenient . . . .
From a notice advertising the foundation of The British School
For Girls, Gateshead, 12th October, 1840

8 Abstracts from a child's school primer 1813

The alphabet

A — is an angel who praises the lord
B — is for Bible, God's most holy word
C — is for Church where the righteous resort
5   D — is for the Devil who wishes our hurt

Arithmetic

At the marriage in Cana in Galilee there were six water pots of stone,
holding two or three firkins a-piece. If they held two firkins, how much
water would it take to fill them? And how much if they held three each?
John Poole, *The Village School Improved*, 1813

Questions

a   What is the motivation for providing this school?
b   What particular doctrinal point is being made by the producers of this
notice?
c   What are the functions of this school?
d   How do both extracts reflect the influence of the voluntary
organisations in the type of education provided?
* e   What were the effects of the involvement of religion in nineteenth-
century education?

9 Religion and Education — The Newcastle Report 1861

While . . . we have deemed it to be a matter of the highest importance to
leave the religious teaching in schools assisted from public funds to the
exclusive decision and control of the managers, we feel ourselves
compelled to notice a serious evil incident to this arrangement. It
5   sometimes happens that in places too small to allow of the establishment
of two schools, the only one to which the children of the poor in those
places can resort, is . . . under regulations which render imperative the
teaching of the Church catechism . . . and . . . attendance . . . at
Church. In such cases it may result that persons of other denominations
10 are precluded, unless at the sacrifice of their conscientious convictions
from availing themselves of educational advantages for their children,
furnished in the part by public funds to which as taxpayers, they
contribute . . . . We believe that the evil may safely be left to the curative

influence of public opinion and will not necessitate a compulsory
15 enactment. Should events prove that we are mistaken, it may be the duty
of the Committee of Council to consider whether the public fund placed
at their disposal in aid of popular education may not be administered in
such a manner as will insure to the children of the poor in all places the
opportunity of partaking of its benefits without exposing their parents to
20 a violation of their religious convictions.

> The Newcastle Report, 1861, ch. 6

Questions

a What dangers were becoming obvious by 1861 in leaving education
to the voluntary systems?
b Why is the government particularly concerned (lines 9 – 13)?
c What implications does the source give for further government
involvement in education?
* *d* Why did the government feel obliged to increasingly involve itself in
education?

10 The Peasant Boy and the Limits of Education 1860

. . . Even if it were possible, I doubt whether it would be desirable, with a
view to the real interests of the peasant boy, to keep him at school till he
was 14 or 15 years of age . . . I venture to maintain that it is quite possible
to teach a child soundly and thoroughly, in a way that he shall not forget
5 it, all that is necessary for him to possess in the shape of intellectual
attainment, by the time that he is 10 years old. If he has been properly
looked after in the lower classes, he shall be able to spell correctly the
words that he will ordinarily have to use; he shall read a common
narrative – the paragraph in the newspaper that he cares to read –
10 . . . he shall write his mother a letter that shall be both legible and
intelligible; he knows enough of ciphering to make out, or test the
correctness of, a common shop bill; if he hears talk of foreign countries he
has some notions as to the part of the habitable globe in which they lie;
and underlying all, . . . he has acquaintance enough with the Holy
15 Scriptures to follow the·allusions and the arguments of a plain Saxon
sermon, and a sufficient recollection of the truths taught him in his
catechism, to know what are the duties required of him towards his
Maker and his fellow man.

> Evidence of Rev. James Fraser, later Bishop of Manchester, to
> The Newcastle Commission, 1860

Questions

a What does the Rev. James Fraser's hypothesis of education imply
about his view of society?
b What social role does he view education as playing?

c How can he be identified with the Established Church (lines 14—18)?
d How inadequate was the provision of elementary education before 1870?

11 Revised Code 1862: Payment by Results

. . . 46. Every scholar for whom grants are claimed must be examined according to one of the following standards . . . .

48	Standard I	Standard II	Standard III
Reading	Narrative in monosyllables.	One of the Narratives next in order after monosyllables in an elementary reading book used in the school.	A short paragraph from an elementary reading book used in the school.
Writing	Form on blackboard or slate, from dictation, letters, capital and small manuscript.	Copy in manuscript character in a line of print.	A sentence from the same paragraph, slowly read once, and then dictated in single words.
Arithmetic	Form on blackboard or slate, from dictation figures up to 20; name at sight figures up to 20; add and subtract figures up to 10, orally, from examples on blackboard.	A sum in simple addition or subtraction, and the multiplication table.	A sum in any simple rule as far as short division (inclusive).

	IV	V	VI
Reading	A short paragraph from a more advanced reading book used in the school.	A few lines of poetry from a reading book used in the first class of the school.	A short ordinary paragraph in a newspaper, or other modern narrative.
Writing	A sentence slowly dictated once by a few words at a time, from the same book, but not from the paragraph read.	A sentence slowly dictated once, by a few words at a time, from a reading book used in the first class of the school.	Another short ordinary paragraph in a newspaper, or other modern narrative, slowly dictated once by a few words at a time.
Arithmetic	A sum in compound rules (money).	A sum in compound rules (common weights and measures).	A sum in practice or bills of parcels.

Revised Code, 1862 (Payment by Results)

a Why did the government feel it necessary to introduce payment by results?

b What effect would such a system have on education?

c What would be the implications for the voluntary system viz-à-viz the increasing involvement of government?

* d Why was education as a social investment such an attractive idea in the nineteenth century?

12   The Education Bill 1902

The Act of 1870 successfully carried out this great if . . . limited object . . . But two unforeseen consequences arose . . . and three considerable omissions made themselves felt as time went on. The first of the two unforeseen consequences was the embarrassment into which the
5   Voluntary Schools were thrown by the rivalry of the rate-aided Board Schools . . . Mr Forster and the Government of that day greatly underrated the . . . cost. Mr Forster contemplated that a threepenny rate would do all that had to be done . . . There was a wholly unexpected expenditure by School Boards . . . and the voluntary schools were
10   subjected to a competition which, however good for education, was certainly neither anticipated nor desired by the framers of the Act of 1870. The second result was that a strain . . . was put on upon local finances . . . through the action of a body responsible indeed to the community so far as regards education, but having no responsibility for
15   general expenditure, which was, of course, in the hands of the local authority. . . .
Let me just enumerate hurriedly the three important omissions . . . In the first place, the Act of 1870 provided no organization for voluntary schools. Board Schools . . . were organized under the School Boards.
20   But voluntary schools . . . were isolated and unconnected . . . The second omission was . . . that there was no sufficient provision for the education of the great staff of teachers required for our national schools. And . . . third . . . our primary system was put in no kind of rational or organic connection with our system of secondary education, and through
25   the system of secondary education, with the University education . . . .
Speech by A. J. Balfour introducing The Education Bill, 1902

Questions

a What two unintended results emerged from the 1870 Act (lines 3 – 16)?

b What areas of education did the 1870 Act leave undefined (lines 18 – 25)?

c How had the shortcomings of the Education Act of 1870 necessitated further state responsibility by 1902?

*   *d*   What were the long term effects of the 1870 Education Act on the voluntary system?

13   The Provision of Secondary Education 1904

The purpose of the Public Elementary School is to form and strengthen the character and to develop the intelligence of the children entrusted to it . . . to fit themselves, practically as well as intellectually, for the work of life. . . . It will be an important though subsidiary object of the School
5 to discover individual children who show promise of exceptional capacity, and to develop their special gifts (so far as this can be done without sacrificing the interests of the majority of the children), so that they may be qualified to pass at the proper age into Secondary Schools, and be able to derive the maximum of benefit from the education there
10 offered them.

Elementary Code, 1904

. . . But a definition of the term 'Secondary School' – which has come to have a recognized meaning in English Education – has become indispensable in order to give to Secondary Schools a definite place in the wide and vague scheme of 'education other than elementary', with the
15 provision and organization of which the Local Education Authorities under the Act of 1902 have been charged, and in respect of which they obtain financial aid and administrative regulation from the Board of Education . . . .

Secondary schools are of different types, suited to the different
20 requirements of the scholars, to their place in the social organization, and to the means of the parents of the age at which the regular education of the scholars is obliged to stop short, as well as the occupations and opportunities of development to which they may or should look forward in later life . . . .

Regulations for Secondary Schools, 1904

Questions

a   In the view of government what should be the clear function of elementary education (lines 1–4)?

b   In what ways were the Local Education Authorities more powerful than the School Boards, which they had replaced?

c   What view of society is apparent in the Elementary and Secondary Codes of 1904 and is it substantially different from the Victorian viewpoint?

*   *d*   Why did the government avoid taking full financial responsibility for, and control of, education?

*   *e*   Was the provision of secondary education inevitable after 1870?

Further reading

E. G. West, *Education and the Industrial Revolution* (1975); P. W. Musgrave, *Society and Education in England since 1800* (1968); J. Stuart Maclure, *Educational Documents, England and Wales 1816—1968* (1973); B. Simon, *Education and the Labour Movement 1870—1920* (1965); J. J. & A. J. Bagley, *The State and Education in England and Wales 1833—1968* (1968).

VII   Agriculture 1760 – 1900

Introduction

As Britain moved further into industrialisation its agriculture had to provide a firm foundation to nourish the workforce. The degree to which developments in agriculture encouraged industrialisation is open to debate. In addition, the Industrial Revolution's initial effect on agriculture in the way of applied science and mechanisation was negligible.

The answer to providing more food lay in the rationalisation of land usage known as the Enclosure Movement. From 1760 to 1800 Parliament passed 1000 such Acts, from 1800–1815 800 Acts. Contemporary reaction to such legislation varied, as did that of historians. A more detailed investigation of the evidence has revealed an important methodological principle, that it is dangerous to generalise on to a national scale from local evidence. The locality of agricultural experience determines the latter's shape and effect.

Agricultural incomes ballooned during the Napoleonic Wars only to be severely deflated by the downward trend in prices by 1815. Wheat prices continued to fall until 1835. Careful research has shown that the effect of this deflation depended very much on the locality, providing more clues to the connection between agriculture and industry and some answers to the puzzle of increased output 1815–35 in spite of 'economic disaster'.

The Repeal of the Corn Laws in 1846 demonstrated finally that they had not been necessary. Foreign competitors were in no position to undercut British wheat. 1846 was followed by a period lasting into the 1870s known as High Farming, when the ideas expounded by James Caird were taken up on a wide scale and agriculture enjoyed considerable prosperity. Farm labourers' wages rose and led to the emergence of Joseph Arch's union and the 'revolt' which stemmed more from high expectations than inadequate pay.

Eventually, foreign competition did begin to bite and the last quarter of the century has been viewed as the 'Great Depression' in British agriculture. The most strident complaints came from those landed interests in a position to influence and command attention. Regional differences are again apparent. There is little doubt, however, that foreign grain and meat did alter traditional agricultural patterns in Britain, heralding the shrinkage of arable estates and the agricultural workforce: one more dimension of the transformation of society in the nineteenth century.

1 The Deserted Village

Sweet Smiling village, loveliest of the lawn,
Thy sports are fled, and all thy charms withdrawn;
Amid thy bow'rs the tyrant's hand is seen,
And desolation saddens all thy green:
5   One only master grasps thy whole domain,
And half a tillage stints thy smiling plain;
No more thy glassy brook reflects the day,
But, chok'd with sedges, works its weedy way;
Along thy glades, a solitary quest,
10   The hollow sounding bittern guards its nest;
Amidst thy desert walks the lapwing flies,
And tires their echoes with unvaried cries.
Sunk are thy bow'rs in a shapeless ruin all,
And the long grass o'ertops the mould'ring wall;
15   And trembling, shrinking from the spoiler's hand
Far, far away thy children leave the land.
    Ill fares the land, to hast'ning ills a prey,
Where wealth accumulates and men decay:
Princes and Lords may flourish or may fade:
20   A breath can make them, as a breath has made;
But a bold peasantry, their country's pride,
When once destroyed, can never be supplied.
        Oliver Goldsmith, *The Deserted Village*, 1770

Questions

a What were the main effects of enclosure as Goldsmith saw it (lines 4−5, 16, 21−2)?

b According to Goldsmith, what effects did depopulation have on the landscape (lines 4, 7−8, 13, 14)?

c To what did Goldsmith attribute enclosure (line 18)?

* d When and where did enclosure result in depopulation of the countryside?

* e Why would the retention of a 'bold peasanty' be regarded as essential to England?

2 Middlesex Enclosure

It may further be observed, that commons are entirely defective in the great article of labour; but no sooner does an inclosure take place, than the

scene is agreeably changed from a dreary waste, to the more pleasing one, of the same spot appearing all animation, activity and bustle. Every man,
5 capable of performing such operations, is furnished with plenty of employment, in sinking ditches and drains, in making banks and hedges, and in planting quicks and trees. Nor are the wheelwright, carpenter, smith, and other rural artificers, under the necessity of being idle spectators of the scene, since abundance of work will be found for them,
10 in the erection of farmhouses, and the necessary appendages thereto; and in the forming and making roads, bridges, gates, stiles, implements of husbandry, etc. Even after a few years, when these kind of temporary exertions are over, by the whole being brought into a regular system of husbandry, it will continue to provide both food and employment for a
15 very increased population.

> John Middleton, *View of the Agriculture of Middlesex*, 1798, p. 109.
> Quoted in M. W. Flinn, *Readings in Economic and Social History*,
> 1964, pp. 82−3

Questions

a What did Middleton see as the major drawback to common land (lines 1−2)?

b What basic change did enclosure bring, in his opinion (lines 4−6)?

c What reason does Middleton have for regarding enclosure as an improvement (lines 14−15)?

* d How widespread was enclosure between 1760 and 1840 and what advantages resulted from it?

* e Do you agree with Middleton that enclosures did not merely provide temporary employment? (Also refer to document 3)

3 The Effect of Enclosure

To sum up, the effects of enclosure were rarely great or immediate. In some instances enclosure came as the last act of a long-drawn-out drama of rural change, and merely put 'finis' to the story. In others it sometimes introduced, but more often accelerated, a similar story of change. As the
5 result of enclosure improved farming spread more rapidly than would otherwise have been the case, larger and more efficient farms were more readily developed, and the long-run decline of the smallholder and cottager hastened and made more certain. Enclosure provides a leading example of the large gains in economic efficiency and output that could
10 be achieved by reorganisation of existing resources rather than by invention or new techniques. Enclosure meant more food for the growing population, more land under cultivation and, on balance, more employment in the countryside; and enclosed farms provided the framework for the new advances of the nineteenth century. But in our

15 period enclosure did not affect the whole country, and even the limited
area that felt its influence was not suddenly transformed.

> J. D. Chambers & G. E. Mingay, *The Agricultural Revolution
> 1750—1880*, 1970, p 104

Questions

a Why do the authors of this extract dismiss the idea of enclosure as a
trauma (lines 2−4)?

b What positive effect do they see as having resulted from enclosure
(lines 5−8)?

c According to the authors, how was economic efficiency achieved
(lines 8−11)?

d What gains in economic efficiency from enclosure are outlined (lines
11−14)?

e Why is it a mistake to think of enclosure as a nationwide phenomenon
in the period 1750−1880 (lines 14−16)?

* f What are the grounds for viewing enclosure as merely one aspect of
agrarian change between 1750−1880?

4 Ride Through Sussex

At about four miles from Petersfield we passed through a village called
Rogate. Just before we came to it, I asked a man who was hedging on the
side of the road how much he got a day. He said, 1s. 6d.: and he told me
that the allowed wages was 7d. a day for the man and a gallon loaf a week
5 for the rest of his family; that is to say, one pound and two and a quarter
ounces of bread for each of them; and nothing more! And this, observe, is
one-third short of the bread allowance in gaols, to say nothing of the meat
and clothing and lodging of the inhabitants of gaols. If the man have full
work; if he get his eighteen-pence a day, the whole nine shillings does not
10 purchase a gallon leaf each for a wife and three children, and two gallon
loaves for himself . . . and this, observe, is a vast deal better than the state
of things in the north of Hampshire, where the day-labourer gets but
eight shillings a week. I asked this man how much a day they gave to a
young able man who had no family, and who was compelled to come to
15 the parish-officers for work. Observe, that there are a great many young
men in this situation, because the farmers will not employ single men at
full wages, these full wages being wanted for the married man's family,
just to keep them alive according to the calculation we have just seen.
About the borders of the north of Hampshire they give to these single
20 men two gallon loaves a week, or, in money, two shillings and
eightpence, and nothing more. Here, in this part of Sussex, they give the
single man sevenpence a day . . . and this is the allowance, settled by the
magistrate, for a young, hearty, labouring man; and that, too, in the part
of England where, I believe, they live better than in any other part of it.

> William Cobbett, *Rural Rides*, 12 Nov. 1825, Vol ii, pp 1−2

Questions

  a What was a 'gallon loaf' (line 4)?
  b On what grounds did Cobbett deprecate the allowance for a labourer (lines 6–8)?
  c To what system was Cobbett referring in lines 13–17? Explain how it operated.
* *d* Why were farm labourers' wages in the south of England so low between 1815 and 1840?
* *e* Why was the single man particularly disadvantaged?

5 Pictures of Distress post 1815

The evidence presented to the commissions of enquiry into agrarian distress has since been more carefully sifted, county by county.[1] This produced the conclusion that the western animal-rearing districts, with counties like Lancashire and Cheshire which embraced or lay close to big
5 urban markets for potatoes and dairy produce, barely suffered 'depression' at all. Agricultural incomes dipped unpleasantly in the rearing counties only in the worst troughs of cereal prices, when demand for their lean stock to fatten on southern and eastern arable farms sank away. Arable men simply had no spare investment funds during the spells of
10 very low prices early in the deflation, for example in 1816 and 1821–23. Later, although the price of wheat did not stagger to its nadir until 1835, farm costs had adjusted downwards as well. This, together with a vigorous response in certain sectors of agriculture, thinned out symptoms of true distress in the later price troughs.
15   . . . Greater descriptive exactitude has begun to uncover the kinds of internal agricultural adjustments which make possible a sketchy resolution of the paradox of the period: how to reconcile with maladjusted drops in prices and costs, which for all the revisionism were undoubtedly biting in some arable areas in some years, the equally certain fact that
20 production continued to climb. The per acre yield of wheat, for instance, rose by 16 per cent from 1815/19 to 1832/36.[2] The total population of England and Wales, which had been 11 004 000 in 1815, reached 14 928 000 in 1836, and this enormous increase was fed . . . with no sustained help from imports and clearly without the per capita con-
25 sumption of foodstuffs falling much . . . .
     E. L. Jones, *The Development of English Agriculture 1815–73*, 1968, pp 12–13

[1] G. E. Fussell & M. Compton, 'Agricultural adjustments after the Napoleonic Wars', *Economic History*, III, 1939
[2] M. J. R. Healy & E. L. Jones, 'Wheat yields in England 1815–59, *Journal of Royal Statistical Society*, Series A, Vol 125

a Which farming areas suffered less after 1815 than others (lines 2—6)?
b Why was the depression in farming easier to bear after 1830 (lines 12—14)?
c What major problem does the historian have to answer about the period 1815—40 (lines 17—20)?
* d How was the growing population of England satisfactorily fed between 1815 and 1840?
* e If the population increased dramatically between 1815 and 1840 why did profits and prices not rise?

6 The Labourer's Lot

The lot of the labourers in the south and south Midlands of England was probably the hardest of all at this period. It was here that the Labourers' Revolt of the 1830s, the rick-burnings and Captain Swing, the savage sentences and transportations, the case of the Tolpuddle Martyrs, had left
5 a heritage of hopeless bitterness, and where the New Poor Law seemed most oppressive. There were fewer alternative occupations open to farm labour, and periods of unemployment were almost inevitable. In Dorset, annual contracts at the hiring fairs were usual, but wages were paid by the week, with nothing on wet days; much of the pay was in kind and the
10 whole family was expected to work on the farm. In Wiltshire and Devon, too, wages were very low, but in Cornwall they were rather higher, for there was other work to be had. No part of Cornwall is very far from the coast with its many little ports, and fishing was a major industry, while there was also tin-mining and slate-quarrying.

C. Orwin & E. Whetham, *A History of British Agriculture 1846—1914*, 1964, pp 80—81

Questions

a According to the authors, which farm labourers were hardest hit between 1815—40 (line 1)?
b Explain the meaning of a) Captain Swing and b) The Tolpuddle Martyrs (lines 3—4).
c How were labourers hired in Dorset (lines 7—9)?
d Why were labourers better off in Cornwall (lines 11—14)?
* e What was the effect of the New Poor Law on these areas which suffered agricultural distress up to 1846?

7 High Farming

The crutch of legislative protection has been swept away. No doubt it was first shortened, and then he was allowed to go about without it for

two or three years till he could accustom himself to do without it. But it
still remains a question among farmers – 'Was he an enemy bent on
5   mischief, or a kind of judicious physician, who did this?'
   The writer . . . observing the fears of his brethren, particularly in the
south, is induced to lay before them . . . a . . . narrative . . . in which
success is comparatively independent of foreign competition . . . .
   The leading principle herein developed will be found to be a greater
10 reliance on green crops, grass, and forage, as contradistinguished from
corn, but by no means exclusive of corn. In connexion with this, the
writer desires to direct attention to the prosecution of a high system of
farming, which enlarges the field of labour and and its remuneration,
leads to the accumulation and economy of manure, and affords the means
15 of applying it to the crops in a far more liberal manner than has heretofore
been thought either necessary or advantageous . . . .
   The modes of management which have heretofore been confined to
farms in the neighbourhood of large towns are now gradually extending
into the remoter parts of the country; and the circle is every year
20 widening within which daily the cultivation of vegetables for sale and the
production of butcher-meat, with a more garden-like management of the
soil, are found to be the most profitable points.
   James Caird, *High Farming under Liberal Covenants the best
   Substitute for Protection*, 1848, pp 5 – 28

Questions

a   To what does the phrase 'crutch of legislative protection' refer
    (line 1)?
b   What fears beset the farmers of the south in 1848 (line 6)?
c   What were the main elements of the system of high farming (line 10)?
d   What were the effects of high farming as outlined by Caird (lines
    13 – 22)?
*
e   Explain why the period of high farming was regarded as an
    agricultural golden age.

8   Agriculture and Industry

The great difference in the rate of wages between the southern and
northern counties is a sufficient proof that the wages of the agricultural
labourer are not dependent on the prices of agricultural produce. A
bushel of wheat, a pound of butter, or a stone of meat, is not more
5   valuable in Cumberland or the North Riding, than in Suffolk or
Berkshire; yet the wages of the labourer in the two former are from 60 to
70 per cent higher than in the two latter counties. The price of bread is not
higher in July and August than in May or June; yet in every agricultural
county, the wages of labour during the period of harvest are increased.
10 Nor are better wages directly the effect of capital; for the poor farmer of

the cold clays of Durham or N'b'land pays 11s. a week, while the large capitalist who cultivates half a parish in South Wilts or Dorset pays only 7s. to his labourer. The higher rate is unmistakably due to the increased demand for labour. This has been greatest in the manufacturing and

15 mining districts of the north, and near the commercial towns and great seaports. . . . The welfare of the agricultural labourer is, more than that of any class in the community, dependent on the continued progress of our manufacturing and mercantile industry.

James Caird, *English Agriculture in 1850—51*, 1852, p 519

Questions

a Why did Caird think that farm labourers' wages were not linked to the price of farm produce (lines 1 — 3)?

b What four examples did Caird cite to give weight to his argument (lines 3 — 14)?

c To what does Caird attribute the level of labourers' wages (lines 13 — 14, 16 — 18)?

d Why should the price of bread be higher in July and August (lines 8 — 9)?

* e What were the direct social and economic effects of industrialisation on agriculture 1815 — 73?

9 The Great Depression: Disaster?

Behind all these changes lay the Great Depression in agriculture of 1873 — 96 and its profound effects on landownership. Most contemporaries saw this as an unparalleled disaster, caused by a run of atrocious weather in 1878 — 9 and again in 1893 — 4, and by a swiftly rising flood of imported

5 foodstuffs, which left English agriculture prostrate. Most historians have agreed with them. The evidence is impressive and appears to admit of little doubt. First American prairie wheat in the 1870s, and subsequently Canadian, Indian, Australian and Argentine wheat, knocked the price of English wheat down from an average of 56s. a quarter in 1867 — 71 to 27s.

10 3d. in 1894 — 8, with a low point of 22s. 10d. in 1894. The price of other grains did not fall by so much as wheat's 50 per cent, but still fell substantially, as did the price of wool. With the perfection of refrigerating techniques the import of frozen and chilled meat grew apace from the middle of the 1880s, and meat prices also fell, while the traditional

15 English breakfast of Danish bacon and eggs was being established at the same time. The effects were to be seen in mounting arrears of rent, bankrupt and ruined tenants, and falling rent rolls: and they were to be seen written across the countryside in a dwindling arable acreage, in farms thrown up, and in land suffered to run to weed and waste.

F. M. L. Thompson, *English Landed Society in the Nineteenth Century*, 1963, p 308 — 9

Questions

a To what did contemporaries apparently attribute the great depression in agriculture 1873−96 (lines 2−5)?

b What is the persuasive evidence in support of contemporaries and historians of the period (lines 6−15)?

c What were the main economic effects of the depression (lines 16−19)?

* d How strong is the evidence that English agriculture suffered a depression 1873−96?

10 The Great Depression: its Incidence

It is clear that the depression has not equally affected all parts of Great Britain. In arable counties, where its presence is most manifest, it has entailed very heavy losses on occupiers and owners of land, in some districts considerable areas have ceased to be cultivated, and there has been
5 a great withdrawal of land from the plough. These features of the crisis have been particularly marked on the strong clays and on some very light soils. Broadly speaking, it may be concluded that the heavier the soil, and the greater the proportion of arable land, the more severe has been the depression.
10 In England the situation is undoubtedly a grave one in the eastern, and in parts of some of the southern, countries. . . . In the pastoral counties of Great Britain the depression is of a milder character, but in most of them the depreciation of the value of livestock between 1886 and 1893, and the persistent fall in the price of wool, have largely diminished farming
15 profits and rents. In districts suitable for dairying, market gardening, and poultry rearing, and in the neighbourhood of mines, quarries, large manufacturing centres, and towns, where there is a considerable demand for farm produce, there has been relatively less depression.
One prominent feature of the depression has been the great contraction
20 of the area of land under the plough in all parts of the country.

> *Report of the Royal Commission on Agriculture*, 1897, Br. Parl. Papers XV, p 20. Quoted in B. W. Clapp, Documents in English Economic History, *England since 1760*, 1978

Questions

a According to the 1897 commission what was the effect of the depression on arable counties (lines 2−9)?

b Which areas of England did the commission reckon to have suffered most (lines 10−11)?

c What districts did the commission identify as having weathered the depression most easily (lines 15−18)?

d What general effect did the depression have on agriculture (lines 19−20)?

* e Explain the uneven incidence of the Great Depression in English agriculture 1873−96.

11 Agricultural Lament

In the face of these advantages, however, the rural labourer has never been more discontented than he is at present. That, in his own degree, he is doing the best of the three great classes connected with the land does not appease him in the least. The diffusion of newspapers, the system of Board
5   School education, and the restless spirit of our age have changed him, so that now-a-days it is his main ambition to escape from the soil where he was bred and try his fortune in the cities. This is not wonderful, for there are high wages, company, and amusement, with shorter hours of work. Moreover, on the land he has no prospects: a labourer he is, and in ninety-
10 nine cases out of a hundred a labourer he must remain. Lastly, in many instances, his cottage accommodation is very bad; indeed I have found wretched and insufficient dwellings to be a great factor in the hastening of the rural exodus; and he forgets that in the town it will probably be worse. So he goes. . . . The fact is, of course, that the youth of this
15 (*Norfolk*), as of other districts, does not wish to learn to plough, even when bribed so to do with prizes, and that here, before long, ploughmen, or any skilled labourers, will, to all appearances, be scarce indeed.

> H. Rider Haggard, *Rural England, being an account of agricultural and social researches 1901 & 1902*, Vol II, pp 545−6. Quoted in B. W. Clapp, *England since 1760*

Questions

a   To what did Rider Haggard attribute the agricultural labourer's discontent at the turn of the century (lines 4−5)?

b   What attractions did he think lured the labourer away from the land (lines 7−8)?

c   What two aspects of rural conditions did Rider Haggard isolate as encouragement to the labourer to leave the land (lines 9−13)?

*   d   The transformation from the rural to an urban society. How meaningful is this summary of social change 1800−1900?

Further reading

E. L. Jones, *The Development of English Agriculture 1815−73* (1968); P. J. Perry, *British Agriculture 1875−1914* (1973); M. W. Flinn, *Readings in Economic and Social History* (1964); J. D. Chambers & G. E. Mingay, *The Agricultural Revolution 1750−1880* (1970); C. Orwin & E. Whetham, *A History of British Agriculture 1846−1914* (1964); F. M. L. Thompson, *English Landed Society in the Nineteenth Century* (1963).

VIII Railways – A New Age?

Introduction

The great Victorian economist, Alfred Marshall, observed, 'the dominant fact . . . is the development not of manufacturing but of the transport industries.' Like any other statement we should not accept this at face value but inquire by what means we can test such a hypothesis.

There had been some improvement in transport before the railways arrived, but both the turnpike system, a system of tolls to be used for road improvement and paid by the road user, and the canal system left a great deal to be desired. The history of railway development is a well known one: they were originally designed to serve collieries and canals. The opening of the Liverpool and Manchester railway was the first to exclusively use mechanical traction, both for passengers and goods. When the advantages of the railway became apparent waves of speculation mania broke out, particularly between 1845–47; during this period the construction of nearly 9000 miles of railway track was authorised by Parliament. The cost was enormous, averaging £40 000 per mile.

It is argued that such a dramatic change in transport was bound to affect profoundly both the social and economic life of the country. The railways' impact on competing transport systems is an obvious area for investigation but its effects on industry and agriculture are more diffuse and difficult to isolate. The self-styled economic historians, applying economic theory to historical events, have argued that the impact of railways upon the economy only had a minimal effect in raising the gross national product. Whether or not this view can be supported, the government found this section of industry important enough to merit legislation in 1840, 1842, 1844, 1858 and 1871, in the teeth of hostile oppposition from the railway interests in Parliament.

The impact of the railway on the quality of life is harder still to determine and in terms of the working classes probably incalculable. Hobsbawm likens the coming of the railways to that of nuclear energy after the Second World War, that is, it was the pre-eminent symbol of the modern age. Not to have a railway in a town was a virtual admission of decline.

1 The Origin of the Railways – Two Views

(a) When George Stephenson was struggling to give utterance to his views on the locomotive before the Committee of the House of Commons, those who did not know him supposed him to be a foreigner. Before long the world saw in him an Englishman, stout-hearted and
5 true – one of those master-minds who, by energetic action in new fields of industry, impress their character from time to time upon the age and nation to which they belong.

'I have fought,' said he, 'for the locomotive single-handed for nearly twenty years, having no engineer to help me until I had reared engineers
10 under my own care.' The leading engineers of the day were against him, without exception; yet he did not despair. He had laid hold of a great idea, and he stuck by it; his mind was locked and bolted to the results.

. . . Watt's invention exercised a wonderful quickening influence on every branch of industry, and multiplied a thousand-fold the amount of
15 manufactured productions; and Stephenson enabled these to be distributed with an economy and despatch such as never been thought possible. They have both tended to increase indefinitely the mass of human comforts and enjoyments, and to render them accessible to all . . . it is to be regarded as the grandest application of steam power that
20 has yet been discovered.

Samuel Smiles, *Lives of the Engineers*, Vol III, 1861, pp 472–3

(b) Of course, transport needs gave birth to the railway. It was rational to have coal-waggons along 'tram-lines' from pithead to canal or river, natural to haul them by stationary steam-engines, and sensible to devise a moving steam engine (the locomotive) to pull or push them. It made
25 sense to link an inland coalfield remote from rivers to the coast by an extended railway from Darlington to Stockton (1825), for the high costs of constructing such a line would more than pay for themselves by the sales of coal which it would make possible even though its own profits were meagre. The canny Quakers who found or mobilised the money for
30 it were right; it paid two and a half per cent in 1826, eight per cent in 1832–33 and fifteen per cent in 1839–41. Once the feasibility of a profitable railway had been demonstrated, others outside the mining areas, or more precisely the north-eastern coalfields, naturally copied and improved upon the idea, such as the merchants of Liverpool and
35 Manchester. . . .

E. J. Hobsbawm, *Industry and Empire*, 1970, p 90

Questions

a   According to Samuel Smiles how did the railways originate?
b   Why should Stephenson have been regarded by some as a 'foreigner' (line 3)?
c   What effect did the railway have on the economy (lines 13–20)?

d According to Hobsbawm how did the railways originate (lin' 24)?

e What was the motive for building the Darlington to S railway line (lines 25 – 6)?

f Were the railways financially successful (lines 29 – 34)?

* *g* Explain the differences in treatment concerning the origins of the railways. Why does their interpretation differ? Which interpretation do you favour?

2 The Advantages of Railways

The travelling is cheaper, safer, and easier. A great deal of traffic, which used to go by other roads, comes now by railway; both time and money are saved, though the length of the journey may often be increased. . . . A regiment of soldiers has been carried by the railways from
5 Manchester to Liverpool in two hours. Gentlemen's carriages are conveyed on trucks by the railway. The locomotives travel in safety after dark. The rate of carriage goods in 10s. per ton; by canal it used to be 15s. per ton. The time occupied in the journey by railway is two hours; by canal it is twenty hours. The canals have reduced their rate by thirty per
10 cent. . . . By railway, goods, such as wines and spirits, are not subject to the pilferage which existed on the canals. . . . More persons now travel on their own business. . . . Coal pits have been sunk, and manufacturies established on the line, giving great employment to the poor . . . thus reducing the number of claimants for parochial relief. . . . It is found
15 advantageous for the carriage of milk and garden produce; . . . The value of land on the line has been considerably enhanced by the operation of the railway. . . .
Annual Register, 1832

Questions

a List the advantages that, the writer claims, railways possessed as a means of transport.

b What military function could the railways serve and of what importance would this be to the government (lines 4 – 5)?

c What privilege is extended to wealthy patrons? Why should this provision have been made (lines 5 and 6)?

d What general effects on the economy and society are claimed by the writer of this extract?

* *e* What effect did the railways have on the existing transport system?

3 Railways and the Working Classes

With regard to the extent of accommodation afforded to the poorer classes by railways, it will be seen . . . that a large third class traffic is carried on by most lines in the manufacturing districts of Yorkshire and Lancashire, in the coal districts of the North, and in Scotland. These lines are in great measure dependent upon third class passengers, who are conveyed by all or nearly all the trains at fares averaging from 1d. to 1½d. per mile. . . .

In fine weather respectable tradespeople, clerks, etc., avail themselves of the third class carriages to a considerable extent; but the bulk of the half million third class passengers who are carried on this railway in the course of the year are strictly the working classes, weavers, masons, bricklayers, carpenters, mechanics and labourers of every description, some of whom used formerly to travel by carts, but the great number by foot. . . .

In one respect a remarkable use has been made of the facilities afforded by railway communication. On the occasion of several strikes, when there was press of work, bodies of workmen have been engaged in London and carried to Manchester. . . .

Upon these main lines of communication it is questionable whether the interests of the proprietors will ever induce them to encourage the development of a large third-class traffic. It is satisfactory, however, to find that there is a growing disposition among railway companies, thus circumstanced, to afford the accommodation of at least one train a day by which the poorer classes may be conveyed at reduced fares.

Report of the Officers of the Railway Department to the President of the Board of Trade, Feb. 1842, *Parliamentary Papers*, XLI, pp 25 seq.

Questions

a How did railway accommodation reflect the structure of Victorian society (lines 2 – 3)?

b In which parts of the country was there a large third class traffic (lines 3 – 4)? Why do you think the provision of third class accommodation was concentrated in these areas?

c Why were the railway companies reluctant to provide third class traffic (lines 18 – 20)?

d What would be the advantage of the provision of third class traffic to:
   i) the working classes (lines 11 – 13);
   ii) the employers (lines 15 – 17)?

* e To what extent would the railways affect the quality of life of the working classes in mid-nineteenth-century England?

4 Railways and Safety

It is very satisfactory to observe, that a marked diminution has taken place in the class of accident, such as collision, arising chiefly from mismanagement or defective arrangements. A great proportion of the accidents

which occurred in the end of 1841, were of this nature, no fewer than 17
accidents having occurred in eight months, from August 1840 to April
1841, from the single cause of collisions by trains or engines overtaking
those travelling on the same line. During the nine months from April
1841 to January 1842 only five collisions of this nature occurred, and
those with one exception unattended with fatal consequences. The
diminution in the number of collisions appears too great to be the result of
accident, and may fairly be attributed in a considerable degree to the
more general adoption of the precautions suggested by the Inspector
General and recommended by this department. . . .

The returns of the past year also show a marked diminution in the
number of serious accidents occasioned by the misconduct of engine
drivers. . . . This result may be attributed partly to the beneficial result of
more extended experience, and of the measures taken by several railway
companies, to raise the character of that important class of men, the
engine drivers, and partly to the salutary example of the prosecutions
which have been instituted.

> Report of the Officers of the Railway Department to the
> President of the Board of Trade, Feb. 1842, *Parliamentary Papers*,
> XLI, pp 15 seq.

Questions

a To what extent had the incidence of railway accidents decreased
between 1840 and 1842 (lines 4−8)?

b What had been the cause of this improved accident record (lines 11−13)?

c What powers did the government have in respect of the safety of the
railways (line 13)?

d Why had the quality of engine drivers improved (lines 16−20)?

* e Why had the government not interfered more directly in the running
of the railways?

5   Railway Discipline

The Shildon drivers engaged and paid their own fireman, provided their
own fuel and oil and were paid by the Company at the rate of $\frac{1}{4}$d. per ton
per mile . . . they considered themselves the kings of the road. . . .The
horse-leaders were a tough and truculent gang, not infrequently
tipsy. Consequently a permanent state of war prevailed upon the line
which not infrequently reduced traffic movement to chaos. . . .

Two horse-drivers refused to allow a steam train to pass them by
entering the loops and forced it to follow them for four miles. On the
same day another driver shunted some waggons so violently that his
horse was pitched out of the dandy cart and fell down the Myers Flat
embankment.

Three horse-drivers left their trains blocking the line at Spring Gardens while they went off to a neighbouring pub for a two-hour drinking session.

L. T. C. Rolt, *The Stockton and Darlington Railway*, c. 1828

<table>
<tr><td>15</td><td>Fines</td><td>s. d.</td></tr>
</table>

15 Fines   s. d.
  1   Employees for being on duty without part or whole of the
Company's Uniform, for each offence   1.0d.
  2   For slovenliness and untidyness on duty, or appearing on
duty in damaged Uniform, for each offence   6d.
20 3   Coming on duty late, for the first five minutes and each successive five minutes   6d.
  4   Engine driver for having used greater quantity of coal or oil than the fixed lb. per mile   Coal 2.6d/Oil 1.0d
These rules to be strictly enforced; . . .

Rule Book Festiniog Railway North Wales, 1876

Questions

a   On what basis were the drivers employed (lines 1 − 3)?
b   What attitude prevailed amongst the drivers (line 3)?
*   *c*   Did the railway owners operate the line exclusively (lines 5 − 6)?
d   What was a dandy cart (line 10)? What does this indicate about the operation of the railways?
e   How rigid had discipline become by the 1870s?
*   *f*   Why did increased discipline become necessary on the railways?

6   The Railway Revolution and its Consequences

The most important event of the last quarter of a century in English history is the establishment of Railroads. . . . As an investment and absorption of capital they are greatly influential for good or evil upon the national prosperity. Of late years it has been a favourite abstract theory of
5   a certain school of politicians, that legislation and government ought to abstain altogether from interference with the employment of capital, and ought to abolish all laws which aim at influencing the direction of such employment. . . . It appears to me that, if the legislature had wisely governed the expenditure of capital upon railways, such a source for the
10   gradual and profitable investment of profits and savings would have been an immense national advantage, whereas allowing the public to rush headlong into undertakings . . . has been productive of great private distress. . . . It seems reasonable to conclude that railroads add considerably to the power and promptness of executive rule. . . . In the
15   matters of police the advantage of them has already been experienced in some important cases.

W. Johnston, *England As It is*, 1851, 1, pp 260−276

Questions

a Why have the railways made such an impact on England (lines 2–4)?

b What is W. Johnston referring to when he writes, 'of late years it has been a favourite abstract theory' (line 4)?

c The article was written in 1851. What episode in railway history is Johnston referring to when he writes, 'allowing the public to rush headlong' (lines 11–12)?

d In what ways are railways important to the 'executive' (line 14)?

* *e* What were the reasons for railway mania and in what way was it 'productive of great private distress' (lines 12–13)?

7 Representation of Railway Interests in Parliament

There are eighty-one directors sitting in Parliament; and though many of those take little or no part in the affairs of their respective railways, many of them are the most active members of the boards to which they belong. We have but to look back a few years, and mark the unanimity with
5 which companies adopted the policy of getting themselves represented in the Legislature, to see that the furtherance of their respective interests – especially in cases of competition – was the incentive. How well this policy is understood among the initiated, may be judged from the fact, that gentlemen are now in some cases elected on boards simply because
10 they are members of Parliament.

> H. Spencer, 'Railway Morals and Railway Policy', reprinted from the *Edinburgh Review*, 1855, The Traveller's Library, Vol 25, 1856

The Railway Interest as Political Pressure Group

Of all the nineteenth-century pressure groups, the railway interest was the most infamous. It had little in common with the landowning and farming interests, with whom it was often in dispute; was not a professional body, like the lawyers; and was often in conflict with other
15 business interests. The railway interest represented big business at its most ruthless and at its most highly organised. The railway companies played a crucial part in the industrial development of the United Kingdom. The rise and fall of railway shares was regarded as a barometer of the country's economic state.
20   . . . in the period before 1868 the unity and strength was more apparent than real. . . . Companies planned together only in emergencies and, as governments were generally reluctant to interfere with them, such emergencies arose infrequently. Indeed the United Railway Companies' Committee of 1867 might have lasted no longer than
25 previous *ad hoc* committees which had withered away after a few years existence. That this did not happen was due to a stream of hostile legislation, actual or projected, which demonstrated the need for a permanent structure to protect company interests.

The steady growth of state intervention in the railway industry after
30   1868 was not the result of a carefully prepared plan, but sprang piecemeal
from the efforts of all governments to deal empirically with different
problems of railway administration.

G. Alderman, *The Railway Interest*, 1973, p 25

Questions

a   Why should the railways wish to have their interests represented in
Parliament?

b   According to Spencer how effective was the railway interest in
Parliament?

c   What does Spencer mean when he writes 'especially in cases of
competition' (line 7)?

d   How does Alderman define the nature of the railway interest in
Parliament (lines 12−16)?

e   Why does Alderman describe the railway interest as 'infamous' (line
12)?

f   How does Alderman suggest the importance of the railways to the
economy (lines 18−19)?

g   Why did the railway interests combine more closely after 1868 (lines
26−28)?

*   h   What 'emergencies' obliged the railway interests to combine?

8   Gladstone and Hudson: The Railways and the State

In 1844 Gladstone, still 'the rising hope of the stern, unbending Tories'
created a select committee to enquire into the railways. His own motives
were quite explicit. He wrote later: 'I was engaged in a plan which
contemplated the ultimate acquisition of the railways by the public, and
5   which was much opposed by the railway companies . . . .'[1]
Since then [canal construction in the eighteenth century] the ideological climate had swung against state control, as transport became more of a
good investment and less of a utility. The railway lobby, already
powerful in Parliament, forced the government to emasculate
10   Gladstone's proposals. The Act . . . eventually passed obliged the railway companies to provide a minimum of one train a day in each direction
on their lines on which the 'parliamentary' fare of a penny a mile would
be charged. The government also got the power to purchase lines which
had been in operation for twenty-one years *after the passage of the Act*,
15   which was, not surprisingly, never exercised.
Yet if we compare the positions of Gladstone and Hudson, is there very
much difference between them? Hudson certainly wanted profits which
Gladstone did not. But both wanted the benefits of an amalgamated and
rationally planned system. During the hearings of the Select Committee

1   John Morley, *Life of Gladstone*, Vol 1, p 198

20 Hudson hinted that he would not object to government regulation of
fares and rates if the government were to sanction further amalgamation.
Nothing further was heard of this, but the suggestion was an anticipation
of the relationship of government and the railways at the end of the
century.
25   Gladstone and Hudson were both overtaken by events. During the
mania and for forty years after, duplicate lines were laid down
throughout the country, and had their effect in lowering charges and
improving standards . . . .
    By the end of the nineteenth century the competitive spirit on the
30 railways was beginning to wear itself out . . . . There was no longer any
big gain to be made from railway investment, they became stocks as safe
as government securities.
    With profits much the same in most companies there was more
pressure towards co-operation in the fixing of rates, and as the railways
35 unified in this respect government intervened to regulate rates in the
national interest . . . .
    In the 1900s full state-ownership began to be discussed, although when
the first major re-organisation came after the First World War (during
which, under an act of 1871, the government took over the railway
40 system) a system of amalgamation in four more-or-less regional groups,
state regulated and eventually state subsidised, was followed instead . . . .
    Open University, *The Industrialisation Process 1830–1914*, A100
Units 29–30, pp 90–95

Questions

a What were Gladstone's intentions in respect of the railways (lines 3–
5)?
b What had changed the 'ideological climate' against state control (lines
6–7)?
c What provision did the 1844 Act make for future railway operations
(lines 10–15)?
d What did Hudson and Gladstone have in common (lines 18–19)?
e Why did the competitive aspects of railway construction begin to die
out towards the close of the nineteenth century (lines 29–32)?
f What sort of relationship finally emerged between the state and the
railways in the twentieth century (lines 37–41)?
* g Why did the government not nationalise the railway network as
many European countries had done?

9 New Economic History and Railways

More than a decade ago trumpets heralded new economic history onto
the academic stage . . . .
    The achievement is impressive. Their research on railways exemplifies
all the virtues now recognised as the hallmarks of new economic history.

5 Hypotheses are well specified and logically consistent; measurement is careful and sophisticated and substantial amounts of new data are generated by collection, collation, and by way of imaginative inference based upon economic theory.

The broad conclusions of the new economic history of railways will
10 surely endure and historians can no longer exaggerate the contribution of railways to economic development. Single innovations, even the accelerated growth of particular industries cannot now be described as leading an economy towards 'take-off' or a 'drive to maturity'. Nineteenth-century growth is once again perceived as multi-factoral
15 and complex; as a process in which no one input can be described as necessary or indispensable. Hyperbole and mono-causal explanations have certainly been checked.

Within the history of transport we now understand more clearly the mechanisms through which a decline in the cost of haulage saved real
20 resources, widened markets, promoted local and regional specialisation and provided producers with access to natural resources. In all these ways railways carried forward a process that probably achieved a decisive breakthrough with canals. In fact one of the most interesting hypothesis thrown up by economic history is that for Western Europe, Russia and
25 the United States natural and artificial waterways probably made a greater contribution to long-term economic progress than their more publicised mechanical rival and that railways made the greatest contribution in substituting for overland transport.

Patrick O'Brien, *The New Economic History of the Railways*, 1977, pp 93–100

Railway effect

Questions

a   What do you understand by the movement known as 'new economic history' (lines 4–8)?

b   What methodological contribution has new economic history made to the estimated importance of railways on the economy (lines 9–11)?

c   What conclusions has this new approach made concerning the contribution of railways to the economy of countries (lines 18–21)?

d   What do the terms 'take-off' and 'drive to maturity' mean (line 13)? Which historian originated the terms?

* e   One method employed by the new economic historian to assess the contribution of railways at a particular point in time is to remove them as a factor of the economic scene and then estimate how the economy would have expanded in their absence. What are the major difficulties in this approach?

Further reading

Michael Robbins, *The Railway Age* (1961); J. R. Kellett, *The Impact of Railways on Victorian Cities* (1967); P. O' Brien, *The New Economic History of the Railways* (1977); G. Alderman, *The Railway Interest* (1973).

IX Depression and Decline?
The British Economy
1870—1900

Introduction

Commenting on the years 1873—86 the Royal Commission on the Depression in Trade and Industry attempted to identify the malaise which they believed existed in the British economy. 'While the share of the aggregate wealth produced in the country which now falls to labour is larger than it was twenty years ago, a corresponding diminution has taken place in the share which now falls to capital: in other words while wages have risen profits have fallen.'

The paradox of depression amidst prosperity did not prevent the Victorian commentators and subsequent historians of the period attaching the label 'Great Depression' to the last quarter of the nineteenth century. Many of the usual criteria of retardation did not apply. The volume of trade and industrial production, in real terms, actually increased, while home investment was at least maintained, although the rates of growth compared less favourably with the rising stars of Germany and the USA.

Nevertheless there is a general consensus amongst historians today and while rejecting the notion of an economic 'watershed', they acknowledge that Britain 'went through an unusual and worrying economic experience'[1] which ultimately led to the erosion of Britain's paramount position. There is a fair measure of agreement as to the timing, 1873—96. Less certain are the causes. The following explanations have been offered:

1   Britain's early start in industrialisation became a hindrance when required to adapt to changed economic circumstances.
2   Our export trade was too narrowly based on a few staple industries.
3   The complacency of British entrepreneurs.
4   The restrictive practices of an organised labour force.
5   A system of education hostile to scientific training and social attitudes averse to 'trade'.
6   A low rate of investment in British industry.
7   The growth of foreign competition.

Different historians emphasise particular factors but they are all agreed that a monocausal explanation is inadequate.

---

1   S. B. Saul, *The Myth of the Great Depression 1873—1896*, 1969, p 54

1 Britain: The First Industrial Nation

Many have suggested that Britain suffered a positive disadvantage from her early start in industrialisation. Theoretically this line of thought is all wrong. The early starter has the greater resources to undertake new investment. The fact that old plant and old locations are actually in existence should be no handicap; capital invested is capital sunk, bygones are bygones and if it pays the newcomer to buy certain plant it pays the older producer to scrap whatever he has and buy the new too. The latecomer may learn from his predecessors, avoid mistakes, take short cuts . . . . This, rather than any statistical illusion, may give him a higher rate of growth but it offers no reason why the newcomer should *overtake* the early starter technologically.

In practice there is more to it. The early starter may find it hard, for institutional or psychological reasons, to break away from old methods and locations; the skills and practices of both management and trade unions may be unsuited to the new industrial environment but be deeply resistant to change . . . .

. . . It is important to remember, however, that Britain retained a wide lead in many industrial sectors to 1914. Most of these had their roots in the industrial revolution; cotton textiles and textile machinery, heavy machine tools, custom-built locomotives, ships and steam engines. Some of them were to go into decline after the war but continued investment in them before 1914 was justified by their relative profitability. Some say that, by so investing, British industrialists were maximising short- not long-run interests, but without an improper use of hindsight it is hard to see any meaning in this. What reason could there be for not investing in cotton mills in 1905 when profits expected and realised up to the war were comparable with any elsewhere? And if Britain was wrong to go on making steel rails because future demand was to be poor, were the countries of South America to go without? . . . Britain was surely right to develop these industries as she did and in fact one of her big problems arose from not keeping up with her competitors in one of them − steel-making. It was unfortunate that this inheritance from the past should lead to so many blind alleys. That, however was a difficulty of the future not a contributor to falling rates of growth before 1914. More serious was that traditions created by these industries were not always conducive to the development of new industries side by side with the old. The lack of interest and of the necessary skill on the part of steam-engine makers in building diesel engines was one example. The inability of engineers raised in craft traditions to undertake the wholesale re-thinking of productive processes necessary to manufacture by mass-production methods was another.

S. B. Saul, *The Myth of the Great Depression 1873−1896*, 1969, pp 44−6

Questions

a Why, theoretically speaking, is an early start in industrialisation not a handicap in later years (lines 1−11)?

b What obstacles might hinder modification of the economic structure of a country (lines 12−16)?

c Why did there appear little need for industrialists to change their strategy before 1914 (lines 17−31)?

d What does Saul mean by 'It was unfortunate that this inheritance from the past should lead to so many blind alleys' (lines 32−3)?

e What does Saul blame for Britain's eventual economic retardation (lines 34−41)?

* *f* How relevant were the newer industries of light engineering and chemicals to the British economy during this period?

2 The Entrepreneur and the Economy: The Case Against

Although little is known about the origins and activities of British business leaders in this period . . . there is ample evidence, in both contemporary and recent literature, to suggest that British businessmen were weighted down with complacency, conservatism and antiquated
5 methods from the 1870s onwards . . . . .

One of the reasons for the slow progress made in both the old and new industries was the lack of appreciation by industrialists of the importance of science and technology and its application to industry. This was particularly true in the case of such science-based industries as iron and
10 steel, chemicals and electric engineering, the progress of which was dependent to a large extent upon scientific and technical expertise. But the fact was that British economic supremacy had been built up by a nation of 'practical tinkerers'[1] and British industrialists were strikingly reluctant to depart from 'rule-of-thumb' methods and seemed even proud
15 of the fact that they carried out little original research or employed few technicians . . . .

The secret of German and American success in machine tools was due to the fact that they concentrated on the production of large quantities of one or two standard tools in large, highly specialised and efficiently
20 equipped plants . . . .

. . . If Britain was behind the times in technique and methods of production she was even further behind the times in her selling methods . . . The weaknesses of the English commercial system were emphasised in the Diplomatic and Consular Reports . . . . Some of the
25 main criticisms included the disinclination of traders to supply cheaper goods . . . .

1 D. Landes, *Entrepreneurship and the Economic Growth*, 1969

... Another frequent complaint made was the scarcity of British trade representatives abroad ... Nor was it unusual for the British travellers, few as they were, to be ignorant of the customs and languages of the countries they represented ... Other criticisms included the poor packing of goods and inadequate credit facilities.

D. H. Aldcroft & H. W. Richardson, *The British Economy 1870–1939*, 1969, pp 141–67

Questions

a In what ways have the entrepreneurs been blamed for Britain's economic decline (lines 6–31)?
b What evidence have Aldcroft and Richardson used to justify their views (lines 23–4)?
c According to the article in what ways had the basis of industrial success changed (lines 12–20)?
* d Why should this change in industrial emphasis handicap Britain?

3 The Entrepreneur and the Economy: The Case Re-examined

Were, then, the four decades preceding the First World War a critical period of entrepreneurship? In the light of our present inadequate knowledge the answer must be 'no'. It was simply that with the development of competitive economies, British entrepreneurial errors and hesitations, *always present* even in the period of the classic Industrial Revolution, became more apparent, and the belabouring of the businessmen who seemed inadequate in their responses mollified the frustrations of those who believed that British industrial supremacy before the mid-1870s was somehow normal and her accelerating relative decline thereafter, abnormal. Rather was it that the whole complex of circumstances that produced British pre-eminence before 1873 was fortuitous. To see the course of British economic development in the nineteenth century in terms of the dissipation of an initial fund of entrepreneurship is untenable. . . .

The one certain conclusion that can be drawn . . . is that there is much to be discovered. . . . Indeed the current paucity of information makes it dangerous even to speak of the 'British entrepreneur'. . . . Over the century there were countless different entrepreneurs in a remarkable variety of trades and industries. . . .

. . . there are many aspects of entrepreneurship in nineteenth-century Britain that can profitably be investigated more deeply: the social, educational and religious backgrounds of entrepreneurs and top management . . . ; the motivations of entrepreneurs and their changes in motivation over time; the longevity of firms in different industries; the influence of institutional arrangements upon entrepreneurial goals; the

relationship between size of firms and marketing possibilities. . . .
P. L. Payne, *British Entrepreneurship in the Nineteenth Century*,
1974, pp 56−8

Questions

a   How does Payne answer the charges of entrepreneurial inadequacies
(lines 1−10)?
b   Why is it 'dangerous even to speak of the "British entrepreneur" '
(line 17)?
c   What needs to be understood about the entrepreneur before he can be
assessed (lines 20−26)?
* d   Why should the entrepreneur have been singled out as a major factor
to explain Britain's economic decline?

4   The Labour Force and the British Economy

. . . Probably the truth of the matter is that outside a few isolated
pursuits, of peripheral significance in so far as the economy as a whole was
concerned, old-fashioned, outright rejection of machinery was a rare
occurrence . . . .
5   On the other hand, it cannot be said that mechanisation was invariably
greeted with enthusiasm by ordinary workers and union leaders
alike. . . . Caution, and perhaps even some hostility, might colour their
utterances, but their strategy was a far cry from total rejection. In essence,
it was one of insistence upon various safeguarding provisions . . . .
10   There were two principal manifestations of restriction of
output . . . These include the notorious, but sometimes exceedingly
subtle, 'ca'canny' or 'go slow'. Secondly . . . the old 'lump o' labour'
idea, or the belief that the amount of work to be done . . . was an
unchanging entity to be divided carefully and equitably among the
15 members of the labour force . . . .
In the end one is left with the impression that although a policy of
deliberate go slow or limitation of output was by and large not part of the
credo of official trade unionism, the rank and file were not altogether
immune from the attractions of such a policy . . . .
20   . . . It was the intrusion of unskilled workers into various British
industries that prompted the more powerful craftsmen-dominated
unions into frantic efforts to hold the line by attempting to force
employers to accept the union view that every new machine or process,
no matter how negligible the skill required, should remain the reserve of
25 the skilled operatives . . . .
. . . rigid adherence to a specific apprentice/journeyman ratio remained a common policy of unions still trying to use apprenticeship as a
protective device in the face of innovation, skill displacements and
invasion by the unskilled, and hence provided additional damning

30   evidence for those who sought to demonstrate that it was trade union obstructionism that prevented the country from reaping the full benefits of technological advance.

        A. L. Levine, *Industrial Retardation in Britain 1880–1914*, 1967, pp 79–101

Questions

a   In what ways could the labour force have been held responsible for contributing to Britain's economic decline (lines 20–32)?

b   To what extent was action official or unofficial (lines 16–19)?

c   Why would trade unions be so anxious to preserve, and provide new, safeguards for their members?

d   Why did this attitude deter technological advance?

* *e*   How important was the Trade Union movement in influencing industrial strategy 1867–1914?

* *f*   How effective was the Trade Union movement in Germany and America?

5   The Public Schools and Industry in Britain after 1870

Public Schools, fee paying and usually boarding, had existed long before the nineteenth century, but it was in the middle and latter part of the century that they expanded. An important cause of this expansion was the support given to them by the richer and more established entrepreneurs

5   who increasingly sent their sons to these schools . . . .

    . . . In fact, far from the industrial classes trying to combat the values of the aristocracy, very often they adopted the received standards and values of aristocratic culture as their own, even though these values were inimical to those very qualities which had made the industrial classes so

10   successful. The upper classes had a strong prejudice against 'trade' and those whose money was too recently acquired . . . .

    . . . there were fundamental characteristics which remained relatively unchanged and were common to most, if not all, of them. First the curriculum, which despite adaption and innovation still retained the

15   classics, . . . as the sun at the centre of its galaxy . . . 'only people who were not gentlemen went in for practical, vocational training at secondary level' . . . .

    It is not that the kind of leadership taught at the schools was necessarily hostile to trading and industrial leadership; it was

20   irrelevant . . . .

    The character of the public schools must also have been strongly affected by the school chapel . . . The more or less specifically Anglican nature of the religion would mirror the traditionally landed and gentry context of the Anglican church at this time, while the ideas of obligation

25   and service to the community were constantly brought forward . . . .

Fine and noble values but not the recipes for commercial and industrial success.

    . . . The small number of those undergoing a public school education at this time, in proportion to the population as a whole, might suggest
30 that these schools could not have had the far reaching effects on Britain's economy that are being claimed. However, the extraordinary inadequacy of English secondary education, which was revealed so clearly by the inquiries of the Taunton Commission, meant that the alternative to the sort of secondary education offered by the public school was, very
35 often, no secondary education at all. . . . The traditional way in which English engineers and industrial managers were trained, by apprenticeship, persisted . . . .

    This meant that there was no reservoir of managerial and technological talent which could supply English industry with new management,
40 which might, even with the existing structure of ownership, have done something to mitigate the harmful effects of the 'absentee industrialist'.

    D. Ward, 'The Public Schools and Industry in Britain after 1870', *Journal of Contemporary History*, II, 1967, pp 37–52

Questions

a   Why did the public system expand in the latter half of the nineteenth century (lines 3–5)?

b   Why did the infusion of the entrepreneurial class into the public system not change the curriculum of these schools (lines 6–11)?

c   Why were the classics regarded as 'the sun at the centre of its galaxy' (line 15)?

d   What role did religion play in education and what effect did this have on commerce (lines 26–7)?

e   Explain what the writer means by describing the public school training in leadership as 'irrelevant' (line 20)?

f   Why did the public school system have 'far reaching effects on Britain's economy' (lines 30–31)?

g   In what ways does this article support Aldcroft's assessment of the entrepreneur's responsibility for Britain's decline?

6   Investment and the Great Depression

    . . . the central causal force in the Great Depression was the relative cessation of foreign lending. In less precise terms the period might be entitled 'What happened when the Railways were built'. Of course, railway-building went on, but never in these decades on a scale sufficient
5 to dominate the British capital market and capital goods industries. Savings moved into other channels – channels less profitable to the investor. The expectations of 1871–73 had encouraged great expansion of plant. Cheap money, new inventions, and the need to reduce costs

carried on the process in the decade that followed. The expected marginal
10 efficiency of capital declined.

The whole economic system conformed to the theoretical consequences of this process. There was no increase in the supply of labour, comparable to that of capital, and money wages fell but slightly. Reduced prices brought the benefits of increased productivity to the
15 working man. Wealth was redistributed favourably to labour, despite the introduction of much labour-saving machinery. The Stock Exchange was slack. It was forced to perform the process of revaluing downwards the capital equipment of the community, as its quasi-rents declined. Businessmen were harassed with falling profit margins and increasingly
20 severe competition. Everywhere they began to search for an escape – in the insured markets of positive imperialism, in tariffs, monopolies, employers' associations. None of these trends advanced far in the Great Depression. But they were symptoms of the general ailment. The capitalist was to have a last fling at a rising interest rate in the capital
25 export boom of the decade before the war.

The irritations of the declining yield on capital which accompany intensive investment were to reach a much greater intensity in the period 1919–1939. In the Great Depression, however, there were still outlets for enterprise that yielded a rate high enough to entice the private lender.
30 The Government was not then forced to assume the role of compensatory monopolist in the capital market; but the lines of future development were clearly forecast. The mid-century blandishments of the profit motive had begun to lose their force.

W. W. Rostow, *British Economy of the Nineteenth Century*, 1948, pp 88–9

Questions

a According to Rostow what caused the 'Great Depression' (lines 1–10)?
b Who benefited from the 'Great Depression' (lines 11–16)?
c What does the author mean by 'its quasi-rents declined' (line 18)?
d What does he mean by the phrase 'the Government was not then forced to assume the role of compensatory monopolist' (lines 30–31)?
e How did businessmen attempt to protect themselves (lines 19–25)?
* f Where was British money invested in the late nineteenth century?

7 Foreign Competition

. . . As far as British exports were concerned there was little ground for complacency. Although the export component of the British economy still remained substantial in these years, the growth of manufactured exports was less rapid than that of either Germany or America or the

5   average for the world as a whole . . . . Between 1899 and 1913, for
example, America and Germany accounted for nearly one-half of the
increase in exports of manufactured products from the major industrial
countries.

    . . . Britain was finding it difficult to penetrate the rich and rapidly
10   expanding markets of industrial Europe and America. In part this could
be explained by the spread of tariff protection in these countries, but the
chief factor was undoubtedly the increasing competition . . . .

    . . . In the more underdeveloped areas of the world Britain's export
performances was weakening . . . . Some of Britain's traditional cus-
15   tomers were beginning to produce the goods they had once bought
from Britain . . . . But to a large extent it was the sale of German and
American products . . . Germany, in particular was extremely successful
and by 1913 she was exporting more than Britain to the primary
producing countries. Only in the markets of the semi-industrial countries
20   did Britain continue to maintain a substantial lead and even this was being
challenged by the early twentieth century . . . .

    The penetration of foreign competitors into the markets of the British
colonies or Empire countries is significant since it was here that British
goods were accorded some degree of preference. The extent of foreign
25   competition should not be exaggerated, however . . . .

    In 1913 Britain was still the largest exporter in the world, though only
by a small margin, whilst her share of total world exports fell much less
dramatically in this period than that for manufactured commodities.

    . . . it might be questioned whether all Britain's losses can be attributed
30   simply to the emergence of new industrial competitors . . . . There is
much to commend the suggestion . . . that they stemmed from internal
deficiencies. A country whose industrial structure is too narrowly based
on a few traditional industries is obviously going to be more restricted as
regards trading opportunities, especially if the pattern of demand
35   changes, . . .

        D. Aldcroft, *The Development of British Industry and Foreign
        Competition 1875–1914*, pp 11–36

Questions

a   Which countries were serious threats to Britain's economic su-
     premacy (lines 1–8)?

b   In which type of market was Britain finding extreme difficulty in
     selling her goods (lines 9–12)?

c   Why was Britain selling less in the underdeveloped areas of the world
     (lines 14–17)?

d   Why was 'the penetration of foreign competitors into the markets of
     the British colonies' significant (lines 22–3)?

e   In retrospect, what was the basic weakness in the British economy
     before 1914 (lines 32–5)?

* *f*   How had Britain's export markets changed between 1870–1900?

8 Did Victorian Britain Fail?

The striking feature of the growth of real product is its rapid growth before 1900 and its sharp deceleration afterwards . . . .

. . . More important, however, is the sustained growth of productivity in the 'seventies, 'eighties, and 'nineties, for it was during these
5   years that the conviction grew on Englishmen that they were falling behind the technology of Germany and, especially, the United States. As far as can be ascertained, however, productivity growth in the United States was of the same order of magnitude as in the United Kingdom: rates of 1 or 1.5 % per year are typical of the American and British
10 economy at the time. Given the uncertainties of the data for both countries, the most precise defensible statement is that there was little cause for alarm in the behaviour of British productivity.

. . . Indeed the failure, to be precise, is Edwardian. Nor is there any evidence that productivity responded to the growth of exports: real
15 exports grew faster in the decade and a half before the First World War than they had since the 'sixties, yet productivity declined. Moreover the correlation between capital accumulation and productivity change on which the demand theory of British failure rests is poor: capital accumulation was low in the 'eighties, for example, yet productivity
20 growth was rapid.

A measure of productivity growth using national aggregates of output, labour, and capital, however is a fragile foundation on which to erect theories of British success or failure. This is not because of the large size of the uncertainties in the data . . . . The difficulty is that even with very
25 good data the range of doubt in the result is large . . . . For example, the measure of productivity grew at 1.2 % p.a. from 1870 to 1900, a respectable pace. If the estimates in 1870 and 1900 of real gross national product, the stock of capital, the labour force, and the shares of capital and labour in national product are incorrect by as little as ±3 %, however, the
30 resulting estimate of productivity change will range from 0.77 % p.a. to 1.62 % p.a., that is, by comparison with the United States, from failure to success . . . .

. . . There was a dip of productivity in the 1900s, but it was too short, too late and too uncertain to justify the dramatic description 'climacteric'.
35 Nor does it support the notion that British businessmen were marking time in the 'seventies onward.

. . . The alternative is a picture of an economy not stagnating but growing as rapidly as permitted by the growth of its resources and the effective exploitation of the available technology.

D. M. Closkey, 'Did Victorian Britain Fail?', *Economic History Review*, 1964, p 446

Questions

a   Explain what Closkey means by the phrase 'the growth of real product' (line 1)?

b How does Closkey argue that 'there was little cause for alarm in the
behaviour of British productivity' (lines 11–12)?

c What was the relationship of productivity to;
   i) exports;
   ii) capital accumulation (lines 13–20)?

d What is the major problem in comparing productivity rates between
countries (lines 24–32)?

* *e* What is the evidence to show that the British economy was
expanding between 1870–1914?

9 British Industrial Growth 1873–96: A Balanced View

Mr Coppock and I were originally in broad agreement in our
interpretation of the so-called 'Great Depression', but in my short note on
this subject in this *Review* (Economic Review) I put forward various
arguments, suggesting that he (and also myself) had previously exag-
5 gerated the UK's 'deceleration' in this period. Mr Coppock now accepts
some of my arguments, and doubts whether the period 'has been
correctly dated and named.' On the other hand, however, he still calls
himself a 'pessimist' . . . .

Obviously there are still some substantial differences between us, but I
10 think it should be made quite clear that we are agreed on the fact of
'deceleration' or 'retardation' in the UK's rate of economic growth after
1870 . . . .

Mr Coppock also agrees with me [that] there was nothing peculiar
about the so-called 'Great Depression' – that it was not a great trough,
15 but part of a longer term process of deceleration lasting up to the First
World War.

. . . Whether the falling prices of the period 1873–96 warrant use of
the term 'Great Depression' is doubtful; the effects were not uniformly
depressive.

20 . . . I suggested in my last article that Mr Coppock had exaggerated
the retardation in the UK's percentage rate of growth by comparing the
figures for 1870–74 with those for 1893–97. . . . I still maintain that it
is misleading to compare figures from the early seventies – years of the
biggest boom in the nineteenth century – with those of 1893–97,
25 beginning in a deep slump . . . .

Another criticism which I made in my last article was that misleading
and unfair comparisons have been made between the percentage growth
rates of the UK and other countries, such as the USA and
Germany . . . . I pointed out that the latter countries were at an earlier
30 stage of economic development, and were experiencing the high rates of
growth that Britain had similarly experienced in the early years of the
Industrial Revolution, whereas in the more 'mature' British economy
the 'innovation effects' of early steam-powered mechanisation were

declining . . . . On this I referred to . . . Professor Nef's
35 thesis . . . 'rates of increase in output or in trade are bound to give an
impression of phenomenal rapidity when we start from almost
nothing.' . . . Mr Coppock criticises this quotation, on the grounds that
it 'appears to beg the question of the time dimension.' . . . Does Mr
Coppock really have to produce the truism that, 'the rate of change per
40 unit of time is crucial' . . . .

It is quite true, as Mr Coppock points out, that quantitively the USA
surpassed the UK in manufacturing output by 1881−85, but he ignores
the large differences in area, resources and population; qualitatively
Britain was still more advanced industrially than the USA and, as Mr
45 Coppock admits, the UK maintained its lead in terms of production *per
capita* until the end of the 1890s, and was still ahead of Germany in
1913 . . . .

I agree with Mr Coppock, however, that by the 1890s Britain was
clearly tending to lag behind the USA and Germany in new industrial
50 developments.

A. E. Musson, 'British Industrial Growth, 1873−96: A Balanced
View', *Economic History Review*, 1964, Vol 17, pp 397−403

Questions

a In what ways does Musson disagree with Coppock (lines 7−8, 20,
41−43)?
b In what areas do they agree (lines 5, 13−16, 48−50)?
c In what specific area does Musson argue that Coppock has misled his
readers (lines 26−40)?
* d Was the 'Great Depression' a short-term phenomenon or merely part
of a long-term decline in the British economy?

Further reading

S. B. Saul, *The Myth of the Great Depression* (1969); D. H. Aldcroft &
H. W. Richardson, *The British Economy 1870−1939* (1969); P. L. Payne,
British Entrepreneurship in the Nineteenth Century (1974); A. L. Levine,
Industrial Retardation in Britain 1880−1914 (1967); D. Aldcroft, *The
Development of British Industry and Foreign Competition 1875−1914* (1968).

X   The New Jerusalem?
The Impact of
Industrialisation

Introduction

I will not cease from Mental Fight
Nor shall my sword sleep in my hand
Till we have built Jerusalem
In England's green and pleasant land
    Preface to *Milton* by William Blake

In the Preface to *Milton*, now more familiarly known as *Jerusalem*, Blake
expressed the hope that Jerusalem could be built in 'England's green and
pleasant land'. Despite the emergence of an urban context rather than a
pastoral one, technological advances appeared to produce a society nearer
to that vision. For other critics, however, the dream had become a
nightmare of exploitation and expropriation.

Industrialisation disrupted traditional patterns of social living. New
constraints were imposed on the one hand whilst horizons were extended
in other directions. Distances were overcome, the range of consumer
products was enlarged and cheapened, and social experiences were
diversified.

On the debit side, industrialisation was accompanied by economic
exploitation and appalling living conditions for some sectors of the
population. This remains true without necessarily positing a pre-
industrial Golden Age of social harmony and higher living standards.
Moreover, the emergence of an industrial society, it was claimed, did
undue spiritual damage. Personal relationships took on a corporate,
commercial and mercenary character. Competition and rivalry replaced
a society which had been based on co-operation. In total the effect was to
produce an imbalance between man and nature for man had become as
mechanical in his responses as the machines he tended. Further apprehen-
sions were expressed at the growing uniformity of society, both in terms
of art which had been enslaved in mass produced copies, and in the
conformity which a mass democracy produced.

Paradoxically, the changing composition of the ruling classes gave the
emergent working classes the opportunity to fight for a share in the spoils
of power. Initially working class activity took the form of semi-legal
organisations and actions. The ruling classes quickly saw the advantage of

enlisting the working classes, once they had proved themselves worthy of attention, in their political wrangles. At the same time, despite the revelations of Booth and Rowntree that poverty was still a phenomenon of the 'richest country' in the world, there was an overall rise in living standards for the majority of people during the nineteenth century.

Above all, what is clearly demonstrated, is the flexibility of British social and political institutions in that they were able to absorb criticism without resort to undue repression. They possessed the ability to adapt to, as well as adopt, the new social phenomena that evolved from an industrial society, even though the motivation for change was opposed, and the motivation for acceptance frequently cynical. The moral dilemmas and concerns are still a matter for contemporary debate for the issues brought into being by the first industrial nation are still in a process of evolution.

1   The Progress of the Nation

It has been argued, by high authorities, that there is under all circumstances a tendency in population to press upon the means of subsistence. If, however, we look back to the condition of the mass of the people as it existed in this country, even so recently as the beginning of the
5   present century, and then look around us at the indications of greater comfort and respectability that meet us on every side, it is hardly possible to doubt that here, in England at least, the elements of social improvement have been successfully at work, and that they have been and are producing an increased amount of comfort to the great bulk of
10   the people. This improvement is by no means confined to those who are called, by a somewhat arbitrary distinction, the working classes, but is enjoyed to some degree or other by tradesmen, shopkeepers, farmers, – in short, by every class of men whose personal and family comforts admitted of material increase. Higher in the scale of society, the same
15   cause has been productive of increase of luxury, of increased encouragement to science, literature, and the fine arts, and of additions to the elegancies of life, the indulgence in which has acted upon the condition of the less-favoured classes directly by means of additional employment it has caused, and indirectly also by reason of the general refinement in
20   manners which has been brought about.

G. R. Porter, *Progress of the Nation*, 1851, p 522

Questions

a   To which theory does Porter refer in the opening of the extract (lines 1–3)?

b   According to Porter, what material progress has been made (lines 9–14)?

c   In what ways, does Porter claim, the quality of life has improved (lines 14–20)?

d Has progress changed attitudes towards society (lines 10−12)?

* *e* If you were attempting to measure 'progress' in Victorian England what areas would you investigate?

2 The World Economy and Science

. . . The economic application of science in the vast improvements of the telegraph, the railroads, and the steamships have changed the whole system of commerce. The effect of this has been to destroy local markets, and to consolidate all into one market − the world. If our landlords and
5 farmers want to know the names of the three persons who have knocked out the bottom of our old agricultural system, I can tell them. Their names are Wheatstone, Sir Henry Bessemer, and Dr Joule. The first, by telegraphy, has changed the whole system by which exchanges are made; the second, by his improvements in steel, has altered profoundly the
10 transportation of commodities by sea and land; and the third, by his discoveries of the mechanical equivalent of heat, has led to great economy of coal in compound engines. By these changes the United States, Canada, India, and Russia have their own corn crops brought to our doors. The effect of these discoveries upon the transport of corn will be realised
15 when I state that a small cube of coal which would pass through a ring the size of a shilling, when burned in the compound engine of a modern steamboat, would drive a ton of food and its proportion of the ship two miles on its way from a foreign port. This economy of coal has altered the whole situation . . . . It has made one grain market all over the world.

L. Playfair, 'Subjects of Social Welfare, 1889', pp 108−9, from W. H. B. Court, *British Economic History 1870−1914, Commentary and Documents*, 1966

Questions

a According to the article what has been the main effect of the 'economic application of science' (lines 3−4)?

b Why has the writer singled out these three individuals as having made the most significant contribution (lines 7−12)?

c How would these technological changes affect the mass of people's lives?

* *d* Referring to the chapters on 'Depression and Decline?' and 'Agriculture' how did the international improvement in the supply of wheat have unfortunate consequences?

3 The New Problem

Here, then, were all the elements of a difficult social problem. The towns were the homes of workmen, once artisans with scope for their instinct to

express and create, who had passed into the impersonal routine of the mill; of men and women with peasant outlook and tradition, accustomed
5 to the peace and beauty of nature, shut up in slum and alley; of immigrants from a land of deadly poverty, bringing their own habits and religion into a society struggling with dirt and torn by sectarian strife. All of these types were being drawn into new associations, creating and receiving the influence of new group atmospheres. We know today how
10 subtle and powerful is the influence of what Mazzini called 'collective intuitions'. The new town had thus to satisfy the spiritual needs of men and women wrestling with the most difficult of all spiritual adjustments, forming a new social mind, disturbed by changes that had destroyed the basis of custom in their lives. The evidence of man's power in the world
15 was impressive and ubiquitous. The contrasts that religion had to justify, the inequalities that culture had to reconcile, were glaring and provocative. How was this society placed for that task? On what did it rely to draw these various elements together in mutual sympathy and confidence?

J. L. & Barbara Hammond, *The Bleak Age*, 1934, pp 40−41

Questions

a According to the Hammonds, what were 'the elements of a difficult social problem' (line 1)?

b What do the writers mean when they refer to society as 'torn by sectarian strife' (line 7)?

c According to the extract why did industrialisation create a 'new social mind' (line 13)?

* d Are the Hammonds opposed to industrialisation?

* e What were 'the contrasts that religion had to justify' and 'the inequalities that culture had to reconcile' (lines 15−16)?

4 Art under Plutocracy

. . . That loss of the instinct for beauty which has involved us in the loss of popular art is also busy in depriving us of the only compensation possible for the loss, by surely and not slowly destroying the beauty of the very face of the earth. Not only are London and our other great commercial
5 cities mere masses of sordidness, filth, and squalor, embroidered with patches of pompous and vulgar hideousness, no less revolting to the eye and the mind when one knows what it means: . . . but the disease, which, to a visitor coming from the times of art, reason, and order, would seem to be a love of dirt and ugliness for its own sake, spreads all over the
10 country, and every little market town seizes the opportunity to imitate . . . the majesty of the hell of London and Manchester . . . . Our civilisation is passing like a blight, daily growing heavier and more poisonous, over the whole face of the country, so that every change is sure

to be a change for the worse in its outward aspect. So then it comes to this,
that not only are the minds of great artists narrowed and their sympathies
frozen by their isolation, not only has co-operative art come to a
standstill, but the very food on which both the greater and the lesser art
subsists is being destroyed; . . . .

What has caused the sickness? Machine labour you will say? . . . If
machinery had been used for minimising such labour, the utmost
ingenuity would scarcely have been wasted on it; but is that the case in
any way? Look around the world, and you must agree with John Stuart
Mill in his doubt whether all the machinery of modern times has
lightened the daily work of one labourer. The phrase labour saving
machinery is elliptical, and means machinery which saves the cost of
labour, not the labour itself . . . the essential aim of manufacture is
making a profit; that it is frivolous to consider whether the wares when
made will be of more or less use to the world so long as any one can
be found to buy them at a price which, when the workman engaged in
making them has received of necessaries and comforts as little as he can be
got to take, will leave something over as a reward to the capitalist who has
employed him . . . .

It is this supposition of commerce being an end in itself, of man made
for commerce, not commerce for man, of which art has sickened . . . .

William Morris, *Architecture, Industry and Wealth*, 1902, from a
lecture delivered at Oxford, 14 November, 1883

Questions

a What does William Morris mean by a loss of 'popular art' (line 2)?

b What impact does he think industrialisation had upon the 'instinct for
beauty' (line 1)?

c Why does he think manufacturers mechanised their factories (lines
20–26)?

d How were workers further deceived as consumers according to
Morris (lines 26–32)?

* *e* Explain carefully Morris's argument that the Industrial Revolution
has 'sickened art' (line 34).

5 The Mechanical Age

What wonderful accessions have thus been made, and are still making, to
the physical power of mankind; how much better fed, clothed and lodged
and, in all outward respects, accommodated men now are, or might be,
by a given quantity of labour, is a grateful reflection which forces itself on
everyone. What changes, too, this addition of power is introducing into
the Social System; how wealth has more and more increased, and at the
same time gathered itself more and more into masses, strangely altering
the old relations, and increasing the distance between the rich and the

poor, will be a question for Political Economists, and a much more
10 complex and important one than any they have yet engaged with.

But leaving these matters for the present, let us observe how the
mechanical genius of our time has diffused itself into quite other
provinces. Not the external and physical alone is now managed by
machinery, but the internal and spiritual also. Here too nothing follows
15 its spontaneous course. . . . Thus we have machines for
Education: . . . a secure, universal, straightforward business, to be
conducted in the gross, by proper mechanism, with such intellect as
comes to hand. Then we have religious machines, of all imaginable
varieties; the Bible Society, professing a far higher and heavenly
20 structure, is found, on inquiry, to be altogether an earthly contri-
vance . . . ; a machine for converting the heathen. . . .

With individuals, . . . natural strength avails little. No individual now
hopes to accomplish the poorest enterprise single-handed and without
mechanical aids; he must make interest with some existing corporation,
25 and till his field with their oxen. In these days, more emphatically than
ever, 'to live, signifies to unite with a party, or to make one'. Philosophy,
Science, Art, Literature, all depend on machinery.

These things, which we state lightly enough here, are yet of deep import,
and indicate a mighty change in our whole manner of existence. For the
30 same habit regulates not our modes of action alone, but our modes of
thought and feeling. Men are grown mechanical in head and in heart, as
well as in hand. They have lost faith in individual endeavour, and in
natural force, of any kind. Not for internal perfection, but for external
combinations and arrangements, for institutions, constitutions – for
35 mechanism of one sort or other, do they hope and struggle.

Thomas Carlyle, *Signs of the Times*, 1829

Questions

a According to Carlyle, what positive contribution has the Industrial
Revolution made to the welfare of the mass of the people (lines
1 – 5)?

b In what way has the Industrial Revolution altered the 'Social System'
(line 6)?

c How has the Industrial Revolution increased the distance between the
rich and the poor (lines 8 – 9)?

d How has machinery affected the spiritual nature of Man (lines 14 –
35)?

* e Why should the emergence of an industrial society produce greater
social conformity?

6 A Wasteful Society

We have won through the horrors of the birth and establishment of the
factory system at the cost of physical deterioration. We have purchased a

great commerce at the price of crowding our population into the cities and of robbing millions of strength and beauty. We have given our
5 people what we grimly call elementary education and robbed them of the elements of a natural life. All this has been done that a few of us may enjoy a superfluity of goods and services. Out of the travail of millions we have added to a landed gentry an aristocracy of wealth. These, striding over the bodies of the fallen, proclaim in accents of conviction the prosperity of
10 their country. . . .

    Blessed indeed are the Rich, for theirs is the governance of the realm, theirs is the Kingdom. Theirs is the power above the throne, for it has been a maxim of British politics that our government should be a poor government, and a poor government cannot contend in the direction of
15 affairs with the imperium of wealth. . . .

    To keep a government poor is to keep it weak. The poor government may resolve to educate, but it will have no means to carry out its resolve; its teachers will be underpaid; its schools inefficient. The poor government may pass Housing Acts; it will but call for better houses that will not
20 come when it does call for them. The poor government may piously resolve to create small holdings; there will be no means to carry out the pious resolve. The poor government may, at periodic intervals, look the question of Unemployment in the face; its legislation will but reflect its poverty, and be in its provisions an acknowledgement that the power to
25 employ, the power to govern, is in other hands.

        L. G. Chiozza- Money, *Riches and Poverty*, 1905, pp 318–21

Questions

a What does the writer mean by, 'We have given our people what we grimly call elementary education' (lines 4–5)?

b According to Chiozza- Money, who has been the sole beneficiary of the Industrial Revolution (lines 6–7)?

c In what way has the composition of the ruling class changed during the nineteenth century (lines 7–8)?

d Why has this state of affairs been reached (lines 16–18)?

 * *e* What general solution do you think the writer would propose to improve the condition of the poorer people and on what grounds would it be opposed?

7 The Gulf Between Classes

There is no town in the world where the distance between rich and poor is so great, or the barrier between them so difficult to be crossed. I once ventured to designate the town of Manchester the most *aristocratic* town in England; and, in the sense in which the term was used, the expression is
5 not hyperbolical. The separation between the different classes, and the consequent ignorance of each other's habits and condition, are far more

complete in this place than in any country of the older nations of Europe,
or the agricultural parts of our own kingdom. There is far less *personal*
communication between the master cotton spinner and his workmen,
10   between the calico printer and his blue-handed boys, between the master
tailor and his apprentices, than there is between the Duke of Wellington
and the humblest labourer on his estate, or than there *was* between good
old George the Third and the meanest errand-boy about his palace. I
mention this not as a matter of blame, but I state it simply as a *fact*.

   Canon Parkinson quoted by Engels and Asa Briggs in *Victorian
   Cities*, 1968, p 114

Questions

a   Why does Canon Parkinson assert that Manchester is 'the most
aristocratic town in England' (lines 3 − 4)?
b   How has the gap between the classes occurred (lines 8 − 9)?
c   Why should this gap between the classes exist in the towns as well as
the factories (lines 5 − 8)?
*
d   If there was greater 'personal communication' between classes before
the Industrial Revolution would it be a 'better society'?

8   The Approaching Democracy

The tendency of the last seven centuries of European history has been to
an equalisation of the conditions of men − an equalisation not so much (in
England at least) of wealth as of physical force, of manners, and of
intelligence. The feeling of subordination − that reverence of the lower
5   classes for the upper, which was at once the cause and justification of
feudal polity − has disappeared; political equality has become a passion in
some countries, legal or civil equality is admitted to be necessary in all.
(Speaking of course, of civilised communities only.). . . . Those things
which are the basis of political power − knowledge and self-respect, and
10   the capacity for combined action − have formerly been possessed by the
few only, are now possessed by the many and among them by persons
who do not enjoy civic privileges, though they feel themselves in every
other respect the equals of those who do, Or, in other words, the social
democracy of progress has outrun its political progress. This is dangerous,
15   because it makes the organs of our political life no longer an adequate
expression of our national will; and because there is nothing more
dangerous than a democratic society without democratic institutions.
The possessors of power ought therefore to admit others to share
it . . . lest class hatreds and jealousies arise, lest the people be alienated
20   from their old institutions, and lest power be at last suddenly and
violently seized by hands untrained to use it. The force of this
view . . . suggests no vague or random extension of the franchise, but
the inclusion of those persons who are already powerful. . . . Once

received within the pale of the Constitution, such persons will learn to
25 give their wishes a legitimate expression through its ancient organs: and
they will themselves become its defenders if it should ever be threatened
by the . . . lower classes.

J. Bryce, 'The Historical Aspect of Democracy' in *Essays on
Reform*, 1867

Questions

a Does the writer regard the Industrial Revolution or the history of
Europe to be an agent of 'equalisation of the conditions of men' (lines
1 – 3)?

b What is the nature of this 'equalisation' (lines 2 – 4)?

c What does Bryce mean by the 'social democracy of progress has
outrun its political progress' (lines 8 – 14)?

d Why is there a need to include others within 'democratic institutions'
(lines 18 – 23)?

e What is cynical about Bryce's motives (lines 23 – 7)?

* *f* Why should industrialised society in the nineteenth century bring
about an extension of the franchise?

9 The Poverty Line 1900

Allowing for broken time, the average wage for a labourer in York is
from 18s. to 21s. whereas, according to the figures given earlier in this
chapter, the minimum expenditure necessary to maintain in a state of
physical efficiency a family of two adults and three children is 21s. 8d., or,
5 if there are four children, the sum required would be 26s.

It is thus seen that the *wages paid for unskilled labour in York are insufficient
to provide food, shelter, and clothing adequate to maintain a family in a state of
bare physical efficiency.* It will be remembered that the above estimates of
necessary minimum expenditure are based upon the assumption that the
10 diet is even less generous than that allowed to able-bodied paupers in the
York workhouse, and that *no allowance is made for any expenditure other
than that absolutely required for the maintenance of merely physical efficiency.*

And let us clearly understand what merely physical efficiency means. A
family . . . must   never   spend   a   penny   on   railway   fare   or
15 omnibus. . . . They cannot save, nor can they join a sick club or Trade
Union. . . . The children must have no pocket money. . . . Should a
child fall ill, it must be attended by the parish doctor, should it die, it must
be buried by the parish. Finally the wage-earner must never be absent
from his work for a single day.

B. S. Rowntree, *Poverty: a study of town life*, 1901, pp 132 – 4

Questions

a   What conclusions has Rowntree reached (lines 6–8)?
b   How has Rowntree arrived at this conclusion (lines 8–12)?
c   How do the meagre wages of the poor constrain their activities (lines 13–19)?
* d   Why would it come as a shock to many Victorians that poverty was still so rife?

10   Art and Manufacture

There appears to us, then, a natural and early connection between the pursuit of the Artist and the Manufacturer. . . . The Artist offers to the Manufacturer the conception which is sure to command the homage of the public; the manufacturer enables the artist to give his conception not
5   merely a local habitation in material reality, but an existence which admits of its being known, appreciated, admired and applauded . . . .

There is . . . nothing derogatory to the highest Art in lending its aid to decorate objects of utility. . . . Artists are public teachers; and it is their duty, as well as their interest, to aim at giving the greatest possible extent
10   and publicity to their instructions.

Now a great but silent revolution has been taking place in the production and reproduction of works of Art for more than a century. The whole tendency of modern invention is to facilitate the multiplication of copies, and to perfect accuracy in copying. Even within our own
15   memory these inventions and discoveries have wrought a wonderous change in their tastes and habits of the people; in their power of appreciating works of Art, and their readiness to concur in securing adequate remuneration to artists . . . .

Let us not be misunderstood; we do not wish artists to become the
20   servants of the manufacturers; we do wish them to become their friends and allies; their partners in educating the people; in improving the tastes, and consequently, the morals, of the community; in developing the intellectual strength and the intellectual resources of the United Empire.

W. Cooke-Taylor from *Art Union*, 1 March, 1848

Questions

a   In what sense does the article argue for a partnership between the artist and the manufacturer (lines 1–6)?
b   In what way have artists a duty to their public (lines 8–10)?
c   What change has taken place in 'the power of appreciating works of art' (lines 11–18)?
d   What danger does Cooke-Taylor point out in the possible partnership between the artist and the manufacturer (lines 19–23)?

e How far did nineteenth-century industrialisation result in the divorce of the artist from his society?

11   The Farm Labourer's Creed

I believe in the landowners and farmers, our kind and generous friends, the authors and conservators of our present condition; in the Labourers' Friend Societies, established for our especial benefit, the promoters every year offering prizes to those of us who beget and rear the greatest number
5   of children, that there may be no lack in the future, of serfs to supply the wants of our masters, and minister to their comfort. I believe it to be to the interest of the landowners and farmers that the toilers of the soil should be kept without the means of education, that they may the more easily keep them in a state of submission to their will and dictates, and
10 regard the formation of school Boards and Secular Education as devices of the 'Evil One'. I believe in the clergy of the 'Established Church', who in the goodness of their hearts condescend to distribute among us soup, coals, and blankets, bought with money collected at the village church and supplemented (sic) by the toilers pence; the loan of baby linen when
15 young serfs are born; and for many other mercies received at their hands being truly grateful.
I believe in the Clergy, for they have preached into us contentment with the station into which we have been called, it being our duty to bear and suffer, and complain not.

Anon., *The Farm Labourer's Creed*, Andover, 1884

Questions

a What is the tone of the extract and why is it written in this way?
b Why are those in power anxious to see a continued rise in population (lines 4–5)?
c In what ways are the agricultural workers kept subservient (lines 6–9)?
d How has the Church assisted in keeping the poor subservient (lines 17–19)?
* *e* Was the agricultural labourer better or worse off in 1900 than in 1800?

12   The Cost of Living 1790–1900

In total, then, the whole period from 1790–1900 saw an increase in the real earnings of the average worker of some $2\frac{1}{2}$ times, and probably a doubling within the . . . period 1830–1900. . . . Britain's productive resources had at last enabled her to realise a standard of life that was
5   unique in time and in place . . . Because of this improvement, and

because of the continuous up-grading of labour from less-skilled to more skilled occupations, there can be little doubt that the worker had gained as much as other classes during the period of late Victorian prosperity. . . . It was against this background of optimism that the
10 revelations of poverty by Charles Booth and Seebohm Rowntree . . . came as such a disagreeable shock. By the standards of the most rigorous measures available to them – a subsistence level defined by reference to the smallest amount of food necessary to support mere physical efficiency – they came to an almost precisely similar conclusion,
15 that 30.7 % of the population of London and 27.8 % of the population of York were existing in poverty. . . . In 1900 . . . one half of all the children of the working classes still grew up in poverty, 1 in 6 babies died before reaching their first year, and 1 in 5 of the population would still look forward to the indignity of a pauper's funeral from the workhouse
20 in which they would end their days.

J. Burnett, *A History of the Cost of Living*, 1977, pp 257–8

Questions

a What material progress was made in the period 1790–1900 (lines 1–3)?
b What gains did the workers make and why (lines 5–9)?
c What conclusions concerning poverty were reached by Booth and Rowntree (lines 14–16)?
d In what other ways could Britain ill-afford to be complacent about the conditions of the poor (lines 16–20)?
*
e In what ways did the British workforce benefit and suffer from industrialisation?

Further reading

J. Burnett, *A History of the Cost of Living* (1977); B. S. Rowntree, *Poverty: a study of town life* (1901); A. Briggs, *Victorian Cities* (1968); R. Williams, *Culture and Society* (1963).